6

This book belongs to:
St.John the Evangelist
Catholic Primary School

The Way, the Truth & the Life Series

Pupil Book

Sr. Marcellina Cooney
& Paul McHugh

CATHOLIC TRUTH SOCIETY
PUBLISHERS TO THE HOLY SEE

Introduction

Welcome to 'The Way, the Truth & the Life' series, Book 6.

In this book God's plan for each one of us unfolds: we are invited to be part of God's kingdom, we discover what it is like and how we can become witnesses of the kingdom today.

In our study, we deepen our understanding of God who came down to earth to show us the WAY to live kingdom values of justice, love, forgiveness. He teaches us the TRUTH about what is really important for this life and life eternal. He gives us the promise of everlasting LIFE through his own death and resurrection.

In order to help us to take an active role in the kingdom of God we think about how we are all called to speak out about injustice. We learn about people across the world who speak up for justice and know that some have been persecuted for doing so in this life but have gained eternal life!

We learn, too, about the Mass and the great gift that Jesus gives us of himself in the Eucharist. When we receive Jesus in Holy Communion he gives us the help and courage we need to be his close friends.

When we study the work of the apostles we learn that they were people with strengths and weakness just like we are. We discover how the Holy Spirit transformed them into people of enormous courage and vision: they knew Jesus could work through them.

The concluding chapter in our book is a reflection on how we are called to serve in the kingdom of God. God has given all of us gifts and talents and we learn how we can receive the fullness of the gifts of the Holy Spirit in the Sacrament of Confirmation.

I hope that you will enjoy your study and become true witnesses of the kingdom of God.

✠ Vincent Nichols, Archbishop of Birmingham

Contents

1. The Kingdom of God

> *Reflect on what the kingdom of God is like*

WHAT IS THE KINGDOM OF GOD?

When you use the word king or kingdom what comes to mind?

A kingdom is a place ruled by a king or queen who makes laws that the people obey in order to live in peace and harmony with each other. The people are loyal to their king or queen.

Within any kingdom there are values, things that people think are good and try to live by, for example, justice, love and honesty.

Imagine a country, let's call it Harmony Island, and its king is called Frederick. He makes the laws and rules that will serve his people.

One day, the island's volcano becomes active and King Frederick persuades the people to evacuate the island. The people scatter to different countries but wherever they are they try to live by the values and laws of Harmony Island while still trying to be citizens of whichever country gave them a home.

In a similar way, Christians are scattered in many different countries but remain loyal to God their king. They try to live by God's values of justice, courage, generosity, faith and compassion wherever they are.

People join the kingdom by accepting God as their king. It is an invisible kingdom; one that grows daily as people enter a relationship with God. Usually this is through baptism.

What is the Kingdom of God like?
Jesus explains in Parables

Everybody likes a good story. Jesus knew that people loved listening to stories so he used a type of story called a parable. A parable is an earthly story with a heavenly meaning. Jesus chose very ordinary things to teach us about his kingdom. For example,

he compared the kingdom of God to a mustard seed, a treasure or a pearl.

Parable of the mustard seed

"It is like a mustard seed which at the time of sowing in the soil is the smallest of all the seeds on earth; yet once it is sown it grows into the biggest shrub of them all and puts out big branches so that the birds of the air can shelter in its shade."

(Mark 4:30-32)

This parable has a much deeper meaning than explaining how a mustard seed grows; it is about how the kingdom of God grows. It started with the coming of Jesus, the King. It grows as people accept his kingship and live by the values of the kingdom.

The kingdom of God started small but has spread throughout the world. So in a similar way, it starts small within us and spreads until Jesus is king of our whole life.

Parable of the yeast

"It is like the yeast a woman took and mixed in with three measures of flour till it was leavened all through."

(Luke 13: 21)

This parable suggests that the kingdom of God was like something that started small and grew quietly and powerfully until it changed things completely.

Parables of the treasure and of the pearl

"The kingdom of heaven is like a treasure hidden in a field which someone has found; he hides it again, goes off happy, sells everything he owns and buys the field.

Again, the kingdom of heaven is like a merchant looking for fine pearls; when he finds one of great value he goes and sells everything he owns and buys it."

(Matthew 13: 44-46)

Jesus is not talking about earthly possessions here. He is saying that when we discover the treasures that God offers us we realise they are worth more than anything else.

Activities

1. Imagine someone is putting together a book on parables. Choose a parable you think should go into this book because of its message about the Kingdom of God. Give reasons for your choice.

2. Study the 'Headline News'.

The Universe
Italian priest gave his life for teenagers
Seven teenagers were saved from drowning by Don Stephano...

THE HERALD
Charity workers in battle to help civil war victims
Church aid workers are facing fierce fighting and horrific conditions to provide aid for helpless victims...

THE CATHOLIC TIMES
- The Taizé Community -
A centre for prayer and song for young people - Find out about us... www.taize.com

The Gazette
'Miracle' cured me - now I want to help others
Crippled by multiple sclerosis for years, until a trip to Knock Shrine led to a remarkable recovery - now she has told her story hundreds of times in Ireland, Britain & USA.

(a) Choose two 'Headlines' and say how these examples show people's commitment to the Kingdom of God.

(b) Choose one of the examples and say how it might have been difficult for the Christian involved to put into practice the kingdom values. (See page 54 Teacher's Book)

Extension

3. (a) Research a local or Catholic newspaper to find other examples of how people put the kingdom values into action.

   (b) Cut out the examples to make a collage with them for the classroom.
   Choose a title for the collage.
   (Some Catholic papers to help you are usually found at the back of the church.)

4. Jesus often started telling a parable with **"The Kingdom of God is like..."**
   Use the same opening to create a simile that reflects an aspect of the kingdom of God that you find helpful.

THE KINGDOM - INVITATIONS

Jesus wants everybody to be part of the Kingdom but not everyone realises how important that invitation is. Jesus told this parable to illustrate what he meant.

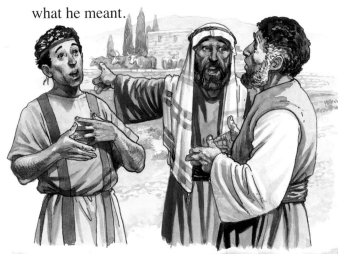

Invited guests who made excuses

"There was a man who gave a great banquet, and he invited a large number of people. When the time for the banquet came, he sent his servant to say to those who had been invited, 'Come along: everything is ready now'. But all alike started to make excuses. The first said, 'I have bought a piece of land and must go and see it. Please accept my apologies.' Another said, 'I have bought five yoke of oxen and am on my way to try them out. Please accept my apologies.' Yet another said, 'I have just got married and so am unable to come'. The servant returned and reported this to his master.

Then the householder, in a rage, said to his servant, 'Go out quickly into the streets and alleys of the town and bring in here the poor, the crippled, the blind and the lame'. 'Sir,' said the servant 'your orders have been carried out and there is still room.' Then the master said to his servant, 'Go to the open roads and the hedgerows and force people to come in to make sure my house is full; because, I tell you, not one of those who were invited shall have a taste of my banquet." (Luke 14:15-24)

As members of the Church we are able to receive help, or grace, to grow in the kingdom of God. This grace is given to us in the sacraments. Each sacrament is like a personal invitation from Jesus.

INVITATIONS to give us...
- **strength,**
- **courage and**
- **grace to live as citizens of the Kingdom.**

In **Baptism** we are invited to join God's family, the Church.
In the **Eucharist** we are invited to receive Jesus.
In **Reconciliation** we are invited to receive God's forgiveness.
In **Confirmation** we are invited to receive the Holy Spirit.

A MEDITATION ON THE OUR FATHER

Our Father in heaven,

you are like an artist and we are the work
of your hands.
We remember the story of your love
and we long to praise and thank you.

We pray that your kingdom may come
to free us from darkness and fear.
We pray that your kingdom may come
to heal our brokenness.

Father, show us that you are near.
Sometimes we feel confused,
trapped by our emotions,
lost or depressed.

Lord, show us what to do.
Teach us to understand your will.

Give us the confidence to thank you
for the comfort of kind friends,
for beauty and bright colours,
for our faith in your love that never ends.

Thank you for the gift of good things to eat.
We are nourished in so many ways by you.

Help us to be forgiving
and bring your bright light to our sleepy souls.
Take our resistance away
that we might build bridges
instead of walls
to bring healing and peace
to the wonderful world you have given us.

Amen

Activities

1. Work in Groups.

   Write or act out a modern interpretation of the parable of the invited guests who make excuses, so as to put across the important message it has for us.

2. Make or design an invitation card to the Kingdom of God that

   (a) would illustrate the importance of the invitation;

   (b) would show who it is from (God).

3. The '**Our Father**' is the great prayer for the kingdom of God.

   On this page, there is a meditation on the '**Our Father**'.

   Use this meditation to make:-

   (a) a classroom display for a '**Prayer Corner**'; or

   (b) a Power Point presentation for an assembly.

   Try to find images and pictures to highlight the meaning.

THE KINGDOM IS FOR EVERYONE

Jesus wants all people to belong to his kingdom. He wants people of every race, culture, age, ability, the good, the bad and the simply not interested.

Even if there is one person missing he will search to find him or her. In order to help us understand how concerned he is about each one of us, Jesus told the parable of the lost sheep.

The Parable of the lost sheep

"What man among you with a hundred sheep, losing one, would not leave the ninety-nine in the wilderness and go after the missing one till he found it? And when he found it, would he not joyfully take it on his shoulders and then, when he got home, call together his friends and neighbours? 'Rejoice with me,' he would say 'I have found my sheep that was lost.'" (Luke 15:4-6)

JESUS IS ALWAYS READY TO FORGIVE

The love Jesus has for each one of us is boundless. He was prepared to give his life for us. Our wrongs do not make him want to disown us. Instead Jesus stands ready to help us to change, if we admit we have been wrong and accept his forgiveness. The stories that follow show how Jesus forgave a woman who had done wrong, a thief and even those who crucified him.

When they heard this they went away one by one until Jesus was alone with the woman. He looked at her and said, 'Woman, where are they? Has no one condemned you?' 'No one, sir' she replied. 'Neither do I condemn you,' said Jesus. 'Go away, and don't sin any more'." (John 8: 1-11)

Jesus pardons the selfish son

Jesus tells the people the parable of the 'Lost Son' to show God's love and mercy. This is the story of the young man who left home, spent all his inheritance and then returned to his father who not only welcomed him back but also had a great celebration.

Jesus forgives the adulterous woman

"One day when Jesus was teaching the people the scribes and Pharisees brought a woman to him; and making her stand there in full view of everybody, they said to Jesus, 'Master, this woman was caught in the very act of committing adultery, and Moses has ordered us in the Law to condemn women like this to death by stoning. What have you to say?' Jesus replied, 'If there is one of you who has not sinned, let him be the first to throw a stone at her'.

Jesus takes the thief to heaven

When hanging on the cross Jesus forgave a thief. This thief was being crucified because he was a criminal. When he saw Jesus on the cross he called out "Jesus, remember me when you come into your kingdom". "Indeed, I promise you," Jesus replied, "today you will be with me in paradise." (Luke 23: 43)

He prays for those who crucify him

When he was dying on the cross Jesus forgave those crucifying him saying "Father, forgive them for they know not what they do". (Luke 23:34)

Activities

1. Read again the section about the Kingdom being for everyone.
   Design a poster to remind people of this.

2. As Christians we accept Jesus as our King.
   Design a logo or badge that expresses your own membership of the Kingdom.

3. 'THE KINGDOM IS FOR EVERYONE'
   This is the title of a web page.

   (a) Show what the rest of the page will look like.

   (b) Remember to include the following: links, images, text and highlight key words.

   (c) **Extension:** Design one of the pages that you'll find on one of the links.

4. (a) Find pictures of the Good Shepherd on the Internet, use www.google.com, click on
      IMAGES and then type 'Good shepherd'.

   (b) Choose one picture to paste into your own work.

   (c) Imagine you are the lost sheep in the picture and write a diary account or a story
      of what happened.

   (d) Make your story show that the Kingdom is for everyone.

Glossary Words

confirmation	The Law	banquet	possessions
condemn	Kingdom values	paradise	scribes
Pharisees	adultery	grace	

USING GOD'S GIFTS TO HELP OTHERS

A TRUE STORY

Vijay was only five years old when he understood that he must look after his mum and dad who could neither hear nor speak.

At this early age he realised he must use his ability to speak and hear to help his parents. He had to tell grown ups that he was in charge - they needed him to communicate with his parents. He was the only one who could answer the telephone or door. He was a thoughtful and mature boy for his age and everybody loved him.

There were times when it was very difficult for Vijay but he seemed to find the strength and courage he needed, even when he felt like giving up. Like Vijay, God has given each of us different talents and skills and he needs us to make full use of them in order to build his kingdom. To help us to understand this, Jesus tells the parable of the talents.

The Parable of the talents

"It is like a man on his way abroad who summoned his servants and entrusted his property to them. To one he gave five talents, to another two, to a third one, each in proportion to his ability. Then he set out. The man who had received the five talents promptly went and traded with them and made five more. The man who had received two made two more in the same way.

But the man who had received one went off and dug a hole in the ground and hid his master's money. Now a long time after, the master of those servants came back and went through his accounts with them. The man who had received the five talents came forward bringing five more. 'Sir,' he said 'you entrusted me with five talents; here are five more that I have made.' His master said to him, 'Well done, good and faithful servant; you have been faithful in small things, I will trust you with greater; come and join in your master's happiness'.

Next the man with two talents came forward. 'Sir,' he said 'you entrusted me with two talents; here are two more that I have made.' His master said to him, 'Well done, good and faithful servant; you have shown you can be faithful in small things, I will trust you with greater; come and join in your master's happiness'." (Matthew 25: 14-23)

In this parable Jesus is making the point that we should use our gifts and talents to promote kingdom values. Whatever abilities we have God has given them to us and he wants us to use them for his service. One day we will have to account for how we have used them. Jesus emphasised that words were not enough but that behaviour and deeds mattered.

Here is another parable Jesus told to show that it is what you do that matters most; words are not enough:

The Parable of the two sons

"A man had two sons. He went and said to the first, 'My boy, you go and work in the vineyard today'. He answered, 'I will not go', but afterwards thought better of it and went. The man then went and said the same thing to the second who answered, 'Certainly, sir', but did not go. Which of the two did the father's will?" (Matthew 21: 28-31)

The religious leaders listening to Jesus had to admit that it was the first son who had obeyed his father, not the one who had said he would. Then Jesus told them that there was a message in it for them because they often promised to obey God and did not do so, while other people who have done wrong say sorry and obey God.

Activities

1. **(a)** Find out what happened at the end of the parable of the Talents (Matthew 25: 24-26).

(b) What do you think this part of the parable means?

2. Create a larger version of this drawing and put in the thoughts, speech and actions of the two sons.

SON1   SON 2

3. Look at the diagram of Kingdom Values.
(See Teacher's Book page 54 for explanations of values)

(a) Write down four of the kingdom values that you think are most important.

(b) Give an example of how each one you have chosen could be put into practice:-

(i) in class,

(ii) in the playground,

(iii) at home.

(c) Share what you have written with the person beside you and then both of you share with two people near you.

(d) In groups create a drama to demonstrate each one.

4. Create an inspirational poster about a kingdom value for display around the school. On the back of it explain what it means to you.

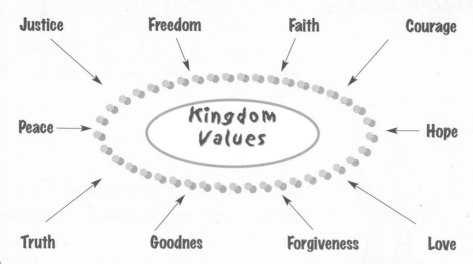

Justice   Freedom   Faith   Courage

Kingdom Values

Peace → Hope ←

Truth   Goodnes   Forgiveness   Love

Glossary Words

justice

talents

freedom

to witness

inspirational

mission

MIRACLES!

When we hear about the miracles Jesus worked we have to try to grasp the reasons behind such actions and what they meant to people at the time.

Jesus was not seeking to make money or fame for himself. He wasn't even trying to stun people into believing in him.

Jesus performed miracles to show the people:

- **what God was like**

- **his compassion for people**

- **who he was (Son of God)**

- **that the Kingdom had arrived**

Jesus can work directly or through people. If we have faith in him we will witness the power of God not only in our own lives but in the lives of other people too.

Do you know the difference between miracles and magic? Magic is an attempt to control forces. Miracles show the power of God working for others.

Disciples have high hopes!

The disciples knew that their leader was unique: he had power to control the elements, cure the sick, change water into wine and even feed 5,000 people with five loaves and two fish.

Those who suffer from dreadful diseases are cured

Jesus controls the storm at sea

The deaf can hear

The disciples were slow to grasp the meaning of the miracles: they believed Jesus would make Israel a great nation. They hoped that he would be a great king in this world and they would have important positions in his kingdom. They even argued about who should get the best positions. (Mark 9:33)

Jesus knew what they were thinking: he knew that they had not understood that it would be an invisible kingdom. The kingdom of God is not about wealth, power and possessions, but rather justice, love and peace here on earth and later in heaven.

When the people witnessed the miracle of Jesus feeding 5,000 with five loaves and two fish, they recognised him as someone who came from God.

Jesus knew that the people were about to take him by force and make him king so he escaped to the hills by himself. (John 6:21)

The people had not understood that the mission of Jesus was to lead people to the kingdom of God, not to build an earthly kingdom.

Activities

1. Jesus performed miracles of three kinds:

   - Power over nature
   - Power over disease
   - Power over death.

   Copy this diagram.

Nature	Disease	Death

   Sort out the miracles below under each heading. You may wish to work in groups of nine and take one miracle each. (See www.tere.org 'Support Material' for copies of materials)

   - Wedding at Cana (John 2:1-12)
   - Miracle of the loaves (John 6:1-14)
   - Cure of the man born blind (John 9:1-7)
   - Calming of the storm (Mark 4:35-41)
   - Healing the paralysed man (Mark 2:1-12)

   - Son of the widow of Nain restored to life (Luke 7:11-16)
   - Cure of the centurion's servant (Luke 7:1-10)
   - Jairus's daughter raised to life (Luke 8:49-56)
   - Resurrection of Lazarus (John 11:1-44)

2. Choose one of the miracles on page 16, write the name of it for a heading and answer the following questions on it:

(a) What words did Jesus use, if any?

(b) What actions did Jesus perform, if any?

(c) What was the result of the miracle?

(d) How did the people react to it?

(e) How did this miracle show the power of Jesus?

(f) What do you think about this miracle?

3. Prepare a '**BEFORE**' and '**AFTER**' tableau (a picture using real people) on a miracle story.

(a) Work in groups and choose one miracle.

(b) Photograph each tableau to capture the meaning for a display.

4. Jesus' miracles show people what God is like. Choose one miracle and write what it tells you about God.

5. Make a mind map of the kingdom of God to show what you know and understand about it. Use a diagram like this to help you:

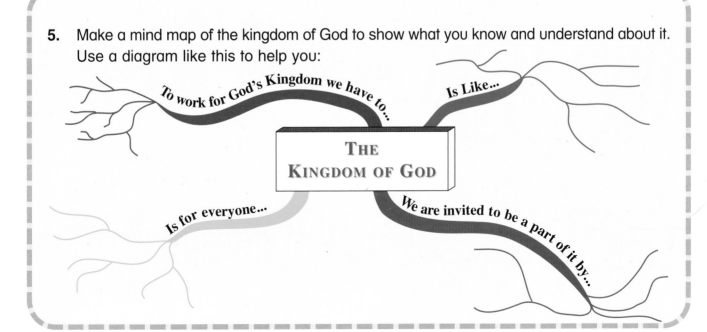

To work for God's Kingdom we have to...

Is Like...

THE KINGDOM OF GOD

Is for everyone...

We are invited to be a part of it by...

2. Justice

Understand what justice is and know that we are called to work for it

JUSTICE

▶ **Justice involves telling the truth**

▶ **It means being fair to others no matter whether they are friends or enemies**

All justice comes from God. God is perfectly just and fair, but he is also perfectly merciful.

He knows that no one in the world is perfectly good, but he can also see inside our hearts and he understands completely all the reasons why we fail to be good. His love and mercy towards us have no end. This is why he sent his Son, Jesus, to save us. But in return, God asks us to work for justice and mercy in the time and place where we are.

"IT'S NOT FAIR"

Think of the number of times you have heard someone say 'It's just not fair!' Sometimes we think that injustice only happens in countries at war or where people are starving. It is easy not to notice that injustice can happen at home, at school or in the area where we live.

Here are some examples:

All during the maths lesson **Fred and John** took it in turns either to chat or knock their pens on the desk - they could see that Miss Connor was getting very annoyed. She told them to stop it several times, but they kept at it - we were all suffering because Miss Connor was cross.

It was Friday afternoon we were all looking forward to games when Mr. Kelly arrived looking very annoyed: 'Who broke the window in the corridor?' Each one of us looked around in search of the guilty person - but no one owned up. So games were cancelled for all of us. (**Class 6**)

There are times when we have to stop and think of how our actions will affect others. It takes courage to be fair to other people and to put their needs before our own - for example, read about the woodcutters and the Himalayan villagers.

The Himalayan villagers

Women living in the hill villages of the Himalayan Mountains of India see the forest as their friend. It provides them with water, firewood and fodder for their animals. The roots of the trees help the earth to keep rainwater all year round which the women then collect from springs and streams.

Unfortunately, other people see the forest as a way of making money and large areas of trees have been sold for industrial use.

When nearby forests are cut down, life for women becomes very hard because they have to walk much further to find water and fuel. In some places where the trees have been cut down heavy rain rushes down the bare hills causing landslides and floods.

One day the villagers discovered that the Forestry Department had sold 300 ash trees to a company making sports equipment.

When the woodcutters arrived the women came to meet them and pleaded with them: "*Brothers, this forest is our shared home. It satisfies so many of our needs. Please do not destroy it …*". There was silence. The men backed off, shame covered their faces.

Eventually they realised how unjust it would be to take what the people needed for their basic needs to provide sports equipment.

Justice means that...

"Everyone has the right to a standard of living adequate for the health and well-being of him/herself and family, including food, clothing, housing and medical care and necessary social services. ...Everyone has the right to education."
(Universal Declaration of Human Rights)

This declaration comes from the United Nations, one of the many organisations promoting justice. However, many people still experience great injustice because of war, poverty, famine or violence.

The following poem describes the injustice faced by those who have to leave their homes.

Refugees

Secretly, we moved forward,
Drawn by dreams of a better life
Leaving our homes
where nothing grows.

It was fear that urged us on
fear of hunger and starvation.
We were stripped at gunpoint
as we neared the frontier.

We carried nothing with us
but memories of love
that bound us together.

Did you know?

About 40 million people die each year from hunger and from hunger-related diseases; over 10 million are children under five. The injustice of this is that there is more than enough food in our world to feed everyone. Over half the people of the world do not have a supply of safe water.

The World Health Organisation estimates that 80% of the sickness and disease in the Third World is caused by lack of access to clean water and sanitation.

'Water, where do I get it?
Oh, from a dirty river two hours walk away.
I do this twice a day.
My brothers and sisters are often ill.'

The injustice is that so much water is wasted in other parts of the world.

People could cut down on their use of water and donate the money saved to CAFOD to provide technical and engineering support to build dams where there is an acute shortage of water.

Activities

1. Read again what has happened in the account of:

- *Class 6*;

- *Fred and John*;

- *Nada*.

In each situation explain:

(a) What is unjust about it?

(b) Who is affected by the injustice?

(c) How it could be put right?

2. Work in pairs:

(a) Describe a situation of injustice that might occur in the playground.

(b) What could be done to help?

3. Imagine you were one of the men who came to the Himalayan villagers to cut down the trees.

Describe how you felt:

- *before*,

- *during, and*

- *after your visit*.

> **Glossary Words**
> **sanitation**

4. Reflect on the poem '**Refugees**'.

(a) Choose a phrase that describes what you think is the greatest injustice they face?

(b) Draw a silhouette of a person and write the phrase you have chosen on it.

(c) Make a display of all the silhouettes and think of a suitable caption to remind us to pray for refugees.

CALLED TO SPEAK!

At times God chooses the most unlikely people to do great things. Some of these people are called prophets. A prophet takes God's message of truth and justice to the people. For example, Moses was chosen to save the Israelites from slavery in Egypt. Jonah was sent to convert the people of Nineveh from their evil ways.

Elijah was another great prophet. He did everything in a big way. Those who believed in God were thrilled with him, but those who did not, found him a terrifying enemy. Read about him in 1 Kings 21 where a man called Naboth was framed for something he did not do.

Today many people are suffering injustice in different parts of the world. God calls us to speak out when we witness injustice.

Sometimes it means defending a pupil who is being treated unfairly by others. On other occasions people are called to make heroic sacrifices to help those who are unable to help themselves.

Each one of us has to be prepared to stand up for the truth and justice, which is what Jesus meant when he said:

"You are the light of the world. A city built on a hilltop cannot be hidden. No one lights a lamp to put it under a tub; they put it on the lamp-stand where it shines for everyone in the house. In the same way your light must shine in the sight of men, so that, seeing your good works, they may give the praise to your Father in heaven." (Matthew 5: 14-16)

Dorothy Day.

Dorothy Day (1897-1980)

Dorothy lived in New York, where many people were unable to find a place to live or work. People were so poor they had no option but to live in the streets. Dorothy knew she had to do something to help them. One day she prayed in front of the Blessed Sacrament in church and pleaded with God to show her what to do.

When she got home a visitor called Peter was waiting to see her. He was one of the poor and homeless but had lots of ideas on how to make life better. "You're a journalist," he said, "We could start a newspaper for the poor." Before long the first issue of 'The Catholic Worker' was sold on the streets of New York, for a penny a copy.

Many people who came to help were homeless. Dorothy remembered the words of Jesus: feed the hungry, clothe the naked and welcome the stranger. She used her last five dollars and rented a flat for six homeless women. It became the first of many 'Houses of Hospitality'.

Dorothy and her friends not only fed the hungry but also stood up for justice. They supported the rights of workers to fair wages and safe conditions in the factories, dockyards and farms of America.

A 'House of Hospitality'.

Dorothy put her beliefs into practice. Whenever the money she needed to buy vegetables for the soup or to pay the rent ran out, she would ask God for what she needed and her prayers were always answered. Her life is an example of how one person, with the help of God, brought hope, comfort and some justice where there was despair.

Activities

1. Draw a story line of Dorothy Day's life, marking important moments, using pictures and symbols.

2. Draw an outline of Dorothy Day. In and around it write what influenced her life.

3. **(a)** Read the story of Elijah and Naboth (Page 56 Teacher's Book or I Kings 21)

   (b) What injustice happened in this story?

4. PRESS CONFERENCE:
   Imagine news has spread about the death of Naboth.
   Journalists arrive to interview all eyewitnesses.

   (a) Nominate pupils to be the journalists and key characters.

   (b) The rest of the class are eyewitnesses.

   • Journalists have to prepare lots of questions to ask. (Some help in Teacher's Book page 58)

   • Eyewitnesses must study the details of the story in advance and keep closely to it when answering questions. (See Teacher's Book page 56 for more information)

   (c) Dramatise one of the scenes and make a video of it or an ICT presentation.

Oscar Romero (1917-1980)

Oscar Romero lived in El Salvador in Central America. He was ordained a priest in 1942 and became Archbishop in 1977.

- He was aware that the wealth of the country was in the hands of a small number of families.

- He saw that the vast majority of people lived in great poverty.

- He knew that the poor lived in hovels made of cardboard and corrugated sheeting, without running water or electricity.

Thousands of people have died and continue to die in El Salvador as they struggle to improve the situation of the poor. Priests and nuns have been tortured and murdered for showing sympathy towards the poor.

Archbishop Romero came to see that the Law of the Land was unjust and evil.

He saw no reason to obey these laws. Even though public meetings were forbidden, he encouraged public demonstrations.

He demanded explanations from the government about the murder of certain priests. He called on Church leaders to become the voice of the poor. He said: *"The world that the Church must serve is the world of the poor."*

It was very clear to all that he was on the side of the poor and those suffering injustice. He even opened his own official residence to the refugees and those hunted for doing good. He allowed a radio station to be set up in the office of the cathedral, which would broadcast the injustice of the government and the powerful wealthy class.

Each Sunday huge crowds gathered for the Mass celebrated by the Archbishop and his sermon was broadcast on the radio. Many people listened in secret, as it was very dangerous to be found out. The government and the army were extremely worried. This archbishop was preaching about the rights of the poor.

Archbishop Romero knew for some time that his life was in danger. About two months before his death he wrote in a Mexican newspaper:

"My life has been threatened many times. I have to confess that, as a Christian, I don't believe in death without resurrection…

As a shepherd I am obliged to give my life for those I love, for the entire Salvadorian people, including those who threaten to assassinate me."

Archbishop Romero was murdered in March 1980 as he was celebrating Mass. At the consecration a shot rang out and he was killed instantly. The spirit of Oscar Romero lives on today in the Salvadoran people: they continue to struggle against injustice as he did. His courage and determination continue to be a source of strength and hope for all.

Dreams come true
Martin Luther King (1929-1968)

He was a black Baptist minister. He was a prophetic voice for all the black people in America who were being treated as second-class citizens. He dreamed of a better world and worked hard to create it. Because he was a Christian he saw his work as a mission from God. Black Americans were kept apart, segregated, from white people. They had to sit in the back seats of the buses; they could not use the same restaurants, parks and swimming pools as the white Americans.

Martin Luther King led a civil rights movement to change these injustices. Thousands of people, black and white, young and old, joined him in protest marches and suffered the violence that was used against them. They were beaten and kicked, had police dogs and fire hoses turned on them, and many were arrested and put in prison. Martin told his supporters to stand up for what was right but no matter what happened, they were never to use violence themselves. He reminded them of what Jesus said:

"Love your enemies. Bless those who curse you. Pray for those who treat you badly." (Matthew 6:44-45)

In 1963, Martin led a march to Washington DC demanding freedom and jobs. A vast crowd heard his most inspiring speech:

"I have a dream that one day men will rise up
and come to see that they are made to live together as brothers.
I still have a dream this morning
that one day every Negro in this country,
every coloured person in the world,
will be judged on the basis of the content of his character
rather than on the colour of his skin,
and every man will respect the dignity and worth of human personality.
I still have a dream today
that one day justice will roll down like water
and righteousness like a mighty stream.

The struggle for civil rights was successful. Segregation was made illegal. Black people won the right to vote. The laws changed but some people still had hatred in their hearts. Martin Luther King was shot and killed by a white racist in 1968. He gave his life in the struggle for equal opportunities and his birthday on 15 January is now a public holiday in the United States.

Activities

Fact File...

1. **(a)** Write as many facts as you can about Oscar Romero.

   (b) Present them in an interesting way, e.g. spider diagram.

   (c) Colour the most important facts and say why they are important.

   (d) If someone asked you why we study Oscar Romero, what would you say?

2. **(a)** Oscar Romero had to cope with many unjust situations. Make a list of the people who are suffering in our community.

   (b) Choose one group and write a prayer for them.

3. Use auto shapes on a computer or draw a dream cloud and write in it your own dream about 'justice' starting with Martin Luther's words:- *'I have a dream...'*

THE GOSPEL MESSAGE

"Go out to the whole world and proclaim the Good News"

(Mark 16:16)

WE are the Church and **we** are called to speak out for:

▸ **JUSTICE (for the poor)**

▸ **COMPASSION (for the weak)**

▸ **RECONCILIATION (for those who have done wrong)**

In different parts of the world there are many people who have responded to Jesus' call to go out and proclaim the Good News. Here is an example:

VIVA RIO! LONG LIVE OUR CITY

How do you turn a city of violence and fear into a place where people want to live? That was the challenge facing *"Viva Rio"*, a campaign by people in Rio de Janeiro, Brazil. They wanted to do something to stop the violence that seemed to be taking over. They knew that in Rio one million out of five million people live in the slums, 'favelas', which climb up the hillsides. Orphan children live in poverty on the streets. Teenage gangs mug and steal from people. Drugs and crime are big problems in Rio. The police use violence to stay in control.

"Viva Rio was born out of passion," says Walter Mattos, a young sports journalist who loves his city. *"Crime was increasing day by day and people were scared. I felt I could not continue to live in this city without doing something to change things."*

Walter contacted business and religious leaders and the daily newspapers. With their support all the people of Rio were invited to keep silent for two minutes and to wear something white as a sign of their desire for peace. The idea took off, and on

17 December 1993 the city came to a halt for two minutes. Traffic stopped and people dressed in white stood still and silent.

Since that day hope has sprung up. There are many new projects. For example, there is support and training to help people get work. Many have started recycling paper and plastics. Very few teenagers had the opportunity to go to secondary school so clubs and churches set up 144 classrooms throughout the city known as "Community TeleSchools".

Each classroom had a television and a video recorder. By attending video courses these young people could complete their education.

The teenagers started to help to make Rio a better place for everyone. Some worked on a project called "Neighbourhood Gardeners" where they planted flowers and helped to care for the city's flowerbeds and squares.

Viva Rio has also tried to cut down on violence by suggesting new methods of community policing. The people were encouraged to give up the weapons they had for self-defence on the streets. *Viva Rio* has shown that by working together ordinary people can improve living conditions for everybody. They can build trust by helping each other and they can turn their city into a place with a hopeful future.

Activities

1. Work in groups to prepare a two-minute presentation on one part of the story of Viva Rio to present to the whole class.

   GROUPS 1 & 2 - Explain the problems in *Viva Rio*.

   GROUPS 3 & 4 - Describe what happened to improve life for the people.

   GROUPS 5 & 6 - Say what you think were the best improvements and why?

Each set of groups come together to agree on what is most important to report back and decide on who is to speak for them.

Glossary Words

convert   racist/racism   sacrifice

segregation   civil rights

Blessed Sacrament

illegal   fair wages   hospitality

Research Project

2. In groups choose one of the agencies listed below and make an interactive display of their work, e.g. 'lift the flap', 'guess what the logo means'.

☞ Give the name of the agency,

☞ what it does,

☞ who it helps,

☞ what you are able to do to help,

☞ how they put the teaching of Jesus into practice.

Group 1

Research how the people who work for CAFOD are helping people suffering from starvation, famine and war.

www.cafod.org.uk/schools/primary/default.asp
Click on the 'Tell us' link to request information.

Group 2

Research how the people who work for Christian Aid are trying to make the world a fair place for all people.

www.christianaid.org.uk

Group 3

Research the work of Pax Christi to find out what it does to help in situations of injustice.

www.paxchristi.org.uk
Telephone: 020 8203 4884
Pax Christi, St Joseph's, Watford Way, Hendon, London NW4 4TY

Group 4

Contact **TEAR**FUND for information on how their members are working for justice in the developing countries.

www.tearfund.org
Tearfund Resources, FREEPOST, Worthing BN13 1BR
Telephone: 0845 355 8355
email: enquiry@tearfund.org

3. Have a 'Prayer Service' for Assembly for all those in need of our support.

(a) Use the prayer of St. Francis: 'Lord, make me an instrument of your peace…'

(b) Recite or sing it using signs to express the meaning of the key words.

(c) You may wish to take each line and say how you can put it into practice e.g. I can bring … where there is …

(d) Use this for assembly or for another class.

ADVENT

Advent is a time when we prepare to celebrate the birth of Jesus who came to bring justice and peace to our world. Throughout the ages prophets have foretold the coming of a great Messiah, a saviour.

Isaiah

The prophet Isaiah said that the saviour would be a person with wisdom and understanding:

> "He does not judge by outward appearances,
> or by what other people say,
> but judges with honesty and truth…"
> (Isaiah 11: 2-4 adapted)

He even saw the day coming when animals who would normally eat each other would become friends:

> "The wolf will sleep with the lamb… the calf and lion cub will eat together… the cow and the bear make friends…" (Isaiah 11: 6-7 adapted)

There will be great rejoicing for those who suffer:

> "Then the eyes of the blind will see,
> the deaf will hear,
> then the lame will jump
> and those who cannot speak will sing for joy…" (Isaiah 35: 5-6 adapted)

The prophet Isaiah also said that another person would come to prepare the way for the coming of the Lord.

JOHN THE BAPTIST

It was John the Baptist whom God chose to prepare the way for Jesus. It was a tough job for John.

He was a wild, fearless character, who lived in the wilderness. He wore a garment of camelhair with a leather belt round his waist, and his food was locusts and wild honey.

He was called to speak out and tell the people they needed to change their ways.

Many people did listen to John and they asked him what they needed to do to be ready for the coming of Jesus. He said:

> "Anyone who has two tunics must share with the one who has none, and anyone with something to eat must do the same." (Luke 3:10-12)

John the Baptist wanted justice for everyone. If he saw wrongdoing he spoke out against it. He even corrected King Herod when he broke the Jewish Law by marrying his brother's wife.

Speaking out against injustice cost John his life on earth but gained him eternal life in heaven. Jesus said there was no greater prophet than John the Baptist.

John has a message for each one of us during this season of Advent. Advent is a time when we make greater effort to get ready on the inside - it's about repenting and having a change of heart. We have to make time to STOP and THINK about our lives and change those things which stop us from being the sort of people God calls us to be.

Advent
is a season when we make a big effort to look at the way we

- ▶ **Treat each other**
- ▶ **Help one another**
- ▶ **Help to promote peace and justice**
  - – In our home
  - – School
  - – In all our relationships

Advent
is a time when we

- ▶ **Make a special place for God in our lives**
- ▶ **Spend time alone with him in prayer**
- ▶ **Celebrate the Sacrament of Reconciliation**
- ▶ **Ask God to send his son Jesus to be with us**

Activities

1. Find out what happened to John the Baptist. (Matthew 14:3-12)

2. **(a)** Make an Advent wreath. You will need:

   - A ring of greenery;

   - Five candles: three purple, one pink and one white.

   (b) On a card write an explanation of what the wreath represents:

   Green wreath represents God's never-ending love for all people,

   Purple candles remind us to prepare our hearts to receive Jesus,

   Rose candle reminds us of the joyful promises Jesus has made.

   White candle represents Jesus among us.

   (c) Light one candle each week when you all pray together.
   The rose candle is for the third week and the white for Christmas.

   (d) Create an information leaflet to explain why we have the Advent wreath.

3. In four groups make preparations for a liturgy for each week of Advent; each group takes a different week and chooses a carol, reading and prayers of petition for those in need, e.g. refugees.

Suggestions for readings:

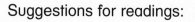

The Annunciation (Luke 1: 26-38)

The Visitation (Luke 1: 39-45)

The Birth of Jesus (Luke 2: 1-8)

The Visit of the Shepherds
(Luke 2: 8-20)

4. Think of two different ways to remind people of the real meaning of Christmas.

5. Think of the different reasons we have for celebrating Christmas.
   Write down four reasons and then put them in order of priority for Christians.

6. Read the story of 'Football in the Snow'. (Teacher's Book Page 60)

   Imagine all the pupils in the class were the British soldiers in the trenches on Christmas Eve. Some of you arrive back home and are surrounded by journalists who want to interview you about your reasons for celebrating Christmas with the enemy.

   (a) Take it in turns to be a soldier or a journalist.

   (b) How were you feeling on Christmas Eve in the trenches?

   (c) What does Christmas mean to you?

   (d) What did you do when the Germans began to sing 'Stille Nacht'?

   (e) Looking back, do you think you did the right thing? Why?

7. Imagine you are a journalist writing a report on the event for the local newspaper.

   (a) Describe what happened.

   (b) Give reasons why many of the soldiers decided to celebrate.

   (c) Say how each one is feeling about it now.

   (d) Say whether you think they acted rightly or wrongly.

8. Imagine that the soldiers are now grandparents. What do you think they would say to their grandchildren about this event?

Glossary Words

compassion	trade union	Messiah	liturgy	eternal life

3. Jesus, the Bread of Life

MEMORIES

What's your most vivid memory? Are there things that remind you of this event?

PEOPLE OF ISRAEL

Every year the Jewish people remembered and celebrated the story of how they escaped from Egypt. When the Israelites (Jews) were slaves in Egypt, God chose Moses to lead them to freedom. However, Pharaoh, (the King of Egypt) was unwilling to let them go free. He received many warnings from Moses, which he ignored, so this is what God told Moses to do.

A SACRIFICE AND A MEAL

Every Israelite family was to choose a perfect male lamb to offer to God in sacrifice. The people of Israel were to cook and eat the flesh of the lamb with unleavened bread and bitter herbs.

Freedom and the promised land

The blood of the lamb was to be put on the doorposts to show where the Israelites were gathered. In this way the final plague which was to strike the land of Egypt would **pass over** them. This is **the Passover**.

Then Moses led the people out of slavery towards the Promised Land.

The waters of the Red Sea divided to allow them to pass through while the Egyptians pursuing them were swallowed up in the waves.

Remembrance

God commanded the people to remember the Passover and celebrate it forever.

Ever since, Jews celebrate the Passover and remember the marvellous events by which God freed the Israelites from slavery in Egypt.

Activities

1. Make a storyboard in order to put the Passover into context.

   Class divides into 4 groups.

   Group 1 – Birth of Moses
   Group 2 – God chooses Moses
   Group 3 – Moses goes to Pharaoh. The plagues God sends on the Egyptians
   Group 4 – Israelites escape from Egypt

   For help: See Teacher's Book 4 pages 44-46. Look up the bible references below, or look up this website:

   http://www.ainglkiss.com /bibst/mos1.htm

   Exodus 2: 1-10   - Birth of Moses

   Exodus 3: 1-12   - God chooses Moses

   Exodus 7, 8, 9 & 10   - Nine Plagues

   Exodus 12   - The Passover and the tenth plague

2. Research, describe and illustrate what the Jews do at the Passover meal in order to show the relationship between memories and celebration.

   Look up the following websites:

   http://torahtots. com/holidays/pesach /pesseder.htm

   www.passover.com

THE LAST SUPPER

The apostles never forgot the last Passover meal they had with Jesus. He told them how much he longed to celebrate this feast with them because this was to be the beginning of the **New Covenant**. This is what happened:

"Now as they were eating, Jesus took some bread, and when he had said the blessing he broke it and gave it to the disciples. 'Take it and eat;' he said 'this is my body.' Then he took the cup, and when he had returned thanks he gave it to them. 'Drink all of you from this,' he said ' for this is my blood, the blood of the covenant, which is to be poured out for many for the forgiveness of sins. From now on, I tell you, I shall not drink wine until the day I drink the new wine with you in the kingdom of my Father'." (Matthew 26:26-29)

Remembrance

This feast became known as the **Last Supper** for the followers of Jesus because it was the day before he was crucified on the cross. At Mass, the priest says the words of Jesus **'This is My Body'** and **'This is My Blood'.** He says these words in the person of Jesus - because he represents Jesus. Each time Mass is celebrated Jesus becomes present on the altar and we are able to participate in this great mystery.

The English word 'sacrifice' comes from a Latin word meaning 'to make sacred' or 'to make holy'. Making something 'holy' means setting it apart for God. **Sacrifice** is about:

- something that is given freely and lovingly;

- something which is worth giving;

- something which will not be taken back.

It is the giving of something to God that makes it holy.

JESUS makes the PERFECT SACRIFICE

In the Old Testament the high priest offered the blood of an animal as a sacrifice, but Jesus gave himself, his own body and blood. When Jesus freely offered his life on the cross, he gave himself in love to the Father as the most perfect sacrifice to take away the sins of the world.

At Mass, the same sacrifice that Jesus made when he offered his life to the Father on the cross on Calvary, is made present again '**in mystery**', that is, truly present but under the sacramental sign of bread and wine. When the priest at Mass says,

'*Let us proclaim the mystery of faith*', this mystery is a truth too big for our minds to grasp. It is the mystery of the sacrifice of Jesus made truly present for us, but under the sign of bread and wine.

When the priest repeats the words that Jesus said at the Last Supper: '*This is my body, this is my blood*', the bread becomes Jesus' body and the wine becomes Jesus' blood. We still see bread and wine - but in faith we believe Jesus is present.

Before Jesus gave his life for us, eternal life with the Father was closed to us because of sin and selfishness - sin and selfishness means that we think only of ourselves. Through his death and resurrection Jesus gave himself for us, and this opened a new way to the Father for us. This **new way** is open to everyone - but we have to choose this **new way** by giving ourselves to Jesus, that is, choosing him as the Way, the Truth and the Life for us and giving ourselves to one another. We have to put into action the words of Jesus 'Love one another as I have loved you'.

In the story of Fr. Maximilian Kolbe we have an example of someone who gave his own life to help another.

We are not necessarily called to give our lives, but to make an effort to think of the needs of others before our own. In this way we join our lives to Jesus.

Maximilian Kolbe

Fr. Maximilian Kolbe, a prisoner in Auschwitz in 1941, is an example of someone who offered his life to save someone else.

Here is what happened:

A prisoner had just escaped from the Auschwitz concentration camp, so the Nazis picked out ten prisoners to be executed. One of them begged to be spared because of his family. At this point Maximilian Kolbe spoke up saying: "*I am a Catholic Priest. I am willing to take his place.*" The Commandant accepted Fr. Kolbe as a substitute and along with nine others he was condemned to die in the starvation cell.

Activities

1. What is similar and what is different between the sacrifice that Fr. Kolbe made and the sacrifice Jesus made?

   Copy the grid below and fill in your answers.

	Similarities	Differences
Jesus		
Maximilan Kolbe		

2. When we do something for other people God accepts it as an offering to himself - a sacrifice - e.g. in time, money or in service of others.

   Write down two examples of sacrifices that could be made by someone your age.

Research

3. **(a)** Find out what Jesus said about the 'Widow's Mite'. (Mark 12: 41-44)

   (b) In what way was the widow's gift a sacrifice?

Glossary Words

unleavened bread

New Covenant

Sacramental sign

memorial

concentration camp

THE PARTS OF THE MASS

GATHERING

We come together as a community to meet Jesus in a quiet place.

The priest greets all present. His greeting proclaims the presence of Jesus with the community gathered together.

He leads us in making the **sign of the cross**.

The **sign of the cross** is a sign that we belong to God - we are God's people and we know that our life should be shaped by God's plan for us.

When we make the **sign of the cross** we place ourselves in the presence of God.

At the beginning of Mass the Priest says:

> The grace of our Lord Jesus Christ,
> the love of God,
> and the communion of the Holy Spirit
> be with you all.

Reply: **And with your spirit**

THE PENITENTIAL RITE

The Penitential Rite is a form of words we use when we ask for forgiveness and healing for any sin that separates us from each other and from God.

We say sorry to God for the times we have hurt others or have done wrong.

The priest invites the people to call their sins to mind, and to repent of them. He may use the following words:

> **Brethren (brothers and sisters), let us acknowledge our sins, and so prepare ourselves to celebrate the sacred mysteries.**

> I confess to almighty God
> and to you, my brothers and sisters,
> that I have greatly sinned,
> in my thoughts and in my words,
> in what I have done
> and in what I have failed to do,
> through my fault, through my fault,
> through my most grievous fault;
> therefore I ask blessed Mary ever-Virgin,
> all the Angels and Saints,
> and you, my brothers and sisters,
> to pray for me to the Lord our God.

THE GLORIA

On Sundays and certain feast days we sing or say the **Gloria** which is a hymn of praise to God. It is like a song of rejoicing in God's goodness.

LITURGY OF THE WORD

Readings from the Old and New Testament form the Liturgy of the Word.

These readings are called the Word of God because God inspired the writers of the Bible.

We have to listen very carefully because God can speak to us through these readings. We can listen to them as if they were stories about the past - for example, the story of the Exodus when the Israelites escaped from Egypt.

This was a story about things that happened in the past. But we don't say this *was* the Word of the Lord.

We believe that God is speaking to us now, through these words.

This *is* the Word of God.

THE GOSPEL

Before the reading of the gospel the priest greets the people with the words:

The Lord be with you.

We reply:

And with your spirit

When the priest says:
A reading from the holy Gospel according to N.

We reply:

Glory to you, O Lord

While saying these words it is a tradition for us to make a little cross ✝ This is done on our forehead, lips and heart asking God to be in our thoughts (head), in out words (lips) and in our heart.

At the end of the Gospel

Priest: The Gospel of the Lord

All: Praise to you, Lord Jesus Christ

HOMILY

The priest then explains to the people what these readings mean and how they can be applied to our own lives. This is called the homily.

THE CREED

We stand to say the Creed. This is a statement of what we believe about our Faith.

BIDDING PRAYERS

This is a time when we pray for all the needs of the Church and the world.

Activities

1. **(a)** Learn the words of the 'I confess'.

   When you think you know them test each other.

   (b) Here are some reasons why we learn prayers off by heart:

   So that:-

   ▸ we can say them with other people;

   ▸ we can say them when we don't have the book;

   ▸ we can say them when we are alone;

   ▸ we can reflect on them at any time.

   List these reasons in order of importance for you.

2. Divide a large circle in four.

   In each section write an example to explain the following phrases from the 'I confess'.

   I have sinned through my own fault:-

   ▸ in my thoughts,

   ▸ in my words,

   ▸ in what I have done,

   ▸ and in what I have failed to do.

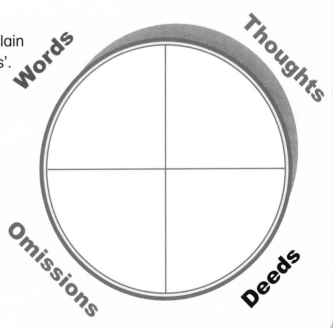

Glossary Words

Proclaim	fellowship	Exodus	Omission

3. Make preparations for a Mass for Ash Wednesday, or in honour of Our Lady.

Work in groups to make a class book 'Preparing for Mass'.

Group 1: Think of the reasons why we make the **sign of the cross** at the beginning of Mass.
Write out the words and underneath explain why we make it.

Group 2: Choose a **Penitential Rite**. Study it and then write your own.
You can add some symbols or pictures to express the meaning.

Group 3: Choose a **reading** from the list your teacher will give you.
Highlight key words. Underneath say why this reading is important.

Group 4: Study the **Gospel** - your teacher will give you the text.
Write an explanation of why you think it is important.

Group 5: Write out some **bidding prayers** for the needs of the Church, the world and the local community.

Group 6: Select some **hymns** that you can sing or a recording that can be played at the beginning, the offertory and at the end of Mass.

OFFERTORY

With humble spirit and contrite heart may we be accepted by you, O Lord, and may our sacrifice in your sight this day be pleasing to you, Lord God.

In the Mass, we bring gifts of bread and wine to the altar. This is because Jesus used bread and wine at the Last Supper. At this point we make, in our hearts, an offering of all our invisible gifts: the work we do in school, the help we give at home and all we do to help others. Jesus unites our offering to his and offers all to the Father.

THE CONSECRATION

At the Consecration, through the action of the priest, the power of the Holy Spirit changes the bread and wine into the body and blood of Jesus with the words '*This is my body*'; '*This is my blood*'.

At this part of the Mass we remember and we take part in Jesus' Last Supper and sacrifice·

AT THE END OF MASS

The priest gives a blessing and says:
*Go forth, the Mass is ended
or Go and announce the Gospel of the Lord
or Go in peace, glorifying the Lord by your life
or Go in peace*
We say: **Thanks be to God**

At the Last Supper Jesus gave the apostles bread and said:

'This is MY BODY'.

Then he gave them a cup of wine to drink and said:

'This is MY BLOOD'

In using these words he meant:

'This is ME'

After that he said:

'Do this in memory of ME'.

We believe the words of Jesus because we know he is God and he can bring about what he says.

THE LORD'S PRAYER

We stand to say the prayer that Jesus taught his disciples. This is the **'Our Father'** or **'Lord's Prayer'**. We have one Father in heaven and we are all his children.

HOLY COMMUNION

At Communion we receive the body and blood of Jesus.

With the priest we prepare by saying:

Lamb of God, you take away the sins of the word: have mercy on us.

Lamb of God, you take away the sins of the world: have mercy on us.

Lamb of God, you take away the sins of the world: grant us peace.

For the Israelites, a lamb was a reminder of something pure and innocent that they offered to God.

Jesus is the reason why we do not sacrifice animals to God. He has replaced all imperfect sacrifices.

Through his **life**, **death** and **resurrection** he is the perfect sacrifice for all time.

In the Mass:

- Jesus is 'the pure and innocent one', without spot or stain of sin.

- Jesus is the gift God gives to us.

- Jesus is the 'Lamb of God'. He is the perfect, absolute gift.

When we go to receive Holy Communion we do not see Jesus with our eyes nor hear him with our ears. But we believe that he comes to us when we receive the sacred Host, the Bread of Life.

AMEN

When we receive Jesus, we say 'Amen'.

'Amen' means 'it is true' and 'I agree'.

To say 'Amen' to the 'Body of Christ' is to say:

- 'Yes, I believe Jesus is present'.

- 'Yes, I will try to be like Jesus'.

- 'Yes, I believe Jesus will give me the strength and courage to stay close to him'.

AT THE END OF MASS

The priest gives a blessing and says:
Go in peace to love and serve the Lord.
We say: **Thanks be to God.**

This means that having received Jesus in Holy Communion we are now able to bring his presence into the world, our home, school, playground, football pitch - in fact, everywhere we go. We become co-workers for Jesus.

Glossary Words

innocent	absolute	host
contrite	Our Lady	pure
consecration	humanity	
divinity	Ash Wednesday	

Activities

1. Imagine someone who is not a Christian has asked you what you mean when you say the words of the 'Our Father'.

   Try to explain the following:

   ▸ Hallowed be thy name.

   ▸ Thy kingdom come.

   ▸ Thy will be done on earth as it is in heaven.

   ▸ Forgive us our trespasses.

2. Design a Mass bookmark.
   Try to think of symbols to match the main parts of the Mass. Here is an example of how you could start.

   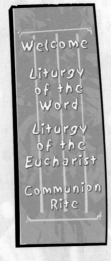

3. The author of the following poem wanted to show what she believed about the Mass.

   (a) Read it slowly and think about the meaning.

   (b) Make notes about your own thoughts on the Mass.

   (c) Use your notes to write a poem, a prayer or a paragraph on the Mass.

MASS

The penitential rite recalls my sin

but if I listen,

with an open heart,

then God's words pour in,

and if I pray for his healing touch

then I feel no fear,

and if I stand in the silence of my soul,

then the offertory draws near.

And then, such power...

The transformation of bread and wine,

a mystery beyond our

comprehension,

a miracle, as they become divine.

So now I stand with an

outstretched hand,

and reach out for what is true.

I long to eat, I want to be complete,

that I might enter into

this communion with you

with my whole being.

Susannah White

ADORATION OF THE BLESSED SACRAMENT

Jesus has promised to be with his Church 'until the end of time'. One of the ways in which he fulfils this promise is through his permanent presence in the Blessed Sacrament.

The Blessed Sacrament is very special to all Catholic churches. It is what we call the consecrated hosts which are kept in the tabernacle, so that we can always pray in the presence of Jesus.

Here are some of the promises Jesus has made to us:

"Whenever two are gathered in my name there I am in the middle of them." (Matthew 18:20)

"I am with you to the end of time." (Matthew 28.20)

"I will not leave you oprhans." (John 14:18)

As the church empties at the end of Mass, Jesus remains. He is truly present - risen and alive.

In Mass, Jesus is Present:

- In the people who are gathered in his name.
- Through the priest who represents him personally.
- In the Word of God read out to all.

  And in a special way...

- In the Blessed Sacrament.

In every tabernacle throughout the world, in tens of thousands of churches and chapels, Jesus waits for us to come to him. He is there to the end of time, as he promised.The Church asks people to show **reverence** (loving respect) for Jesus in the Blessed Sacrament. That is why Catholics **genuflect** (go down on one knee) towards the tabernacle and try to be very quiet.

THE MONSTRANCE

This is a **monstrance**. At special times, the Blessed Sacrament is **exposed** for **Adoration**. People **genuflect** on both knees and bow their heads in **reverence**.

The Church asks people to adore (give loving attention to) Jesus in the Blessed Sacrament.

Spending a few moments of quiet time with Jesus will give us strength and courage. We can start now.

Think of the crowds who gather to try and see film stars and musicians.

Think of the thousands of churches where Jesus is truly present and waits for us.

Activities

1. **(a)** Using the glossary, look up and write out the meaning of the following words:

   Genuflect; Monstrance; Sanctuary Lamp; Tabernacle.

A B C D

(b) Now write down what the pictures A to D are, explaining how you know that each of these indicates that Jesus is present.

Activities

2. Luisa, Tomek and Vikram enter a church.

    (i) Luisa genuflects towards the altar straight ahead.

    (ii) Tomek genuflects towards the crucifix to the left.

    (iii) Vikram genuflects towards the tabernacle to the right.

  (a) Which of the three best understands the reason for genuflecting?

  (b) What is that reason?

3. Choose a hymn about the Blessed Sacrament.

  (a) In what ways do the words speak to us of the Presence of Jesus.

  (b) If the music is available listen to it as you read the words.

  (c) How do the music and the words work together to communicate the Presence of Jesus.

4. Why do you think a quiet atmosphere is important **before**, **during** and **after** Mass?

Glossary Words

hallowed   appearance

trespasses   tabernacle

reverence   expose/exposition

genuflect   altar

adoration   sanctuary lamp

monstrance   crucifix

4. Jesus, Son of God

Know that Jesus' miracles led many to believe he was the Son of God
Reflect on what this means for us

WHAT DOES IT MEAN TO SAY JESUS IS GOD'S SON?

Jesus is 'God-made-man'. He is truly God and as man he is truly human. So when we think of Jesus we are also thinking of God. Through Jesus we know what God is like.

Jesus said: 'To have seen me is to have seen the Father'. (John 14:9)

People did not understand what Jesus meant when he said 'To have seen me is to have seen the Father'. They did not understand that he was truly divine and truly human. In order to help the people **believe** in the **mystery** of his **incarnation**, that is, to believe that he is both God and man Jesus worked many miracles. For example, he healed the sick, restored sight to the blind, raised the dead, changed water into wine, calmed the storm at sea and even walked on water!

Jesus preached the good news to the poor and fed the hungry

Jesus showed his power over nature by walking on water

Miracles of Jesus

We use the word 'miracle' in everyday life. Does it mean the same when we speak of Jesus' miracles? In one sense, yes - the miracles of Jesus were amazing, they made people sit up and take notice. In another sense, no - the miracles of Jesus were not magic tricks or incredible coincidences. They were special signs of God's power alive in Jesus, the God-man. They were also little sneak previews - trailers - of the unfolding victory of the Kingdom of God.

How many miracles did Jesus work?

Hundreds, maybe thousands! Certainly, he worked many more miracles than could be mentioned. Sometimes, the Gospel writers tell us, when Jesus went to a certain village, the people brought all their sick ones from all around that area.

The Gospel writers simply say that 'as many who touched him were cured'.

Why did Jesus work miracles?

Jesus performed miracles for a number of reasons. Here are two of them:

● Out of compassion for people's suffering.

● To show he was the Son of God and to reward people for their faith in him.

For example, a man with leprosy came to Jesus and pleaded on his knees:

'If you want to' he said 'you can cure me'. Feeling sorry for him, Jesus stretched out his hand and touched him. 'Of course I want to! Be cured!

(Mark 1:40-42)

Seeing their faith, Jesus said to the paralytic, 'My child, your sins are forgiven.' Some people grumbled at this; after all, only God could forgive sins, so in order to strengthen their belief in him, he said to the paralytic, 'I order you: get up, pick up your stretcher, and go off home.' So to prove to the people that he was the Son of God he **cured** the man both **spiritually** and **physically**.

(Mark 2: 1-12)

Another example is when Jesus was preaching in a house, some men lowered a man who was paralysed down through the roof.

Miracles were 'glimpses' of the Kingdom - a place where there will be no more sickness, sadness or death.

Did everyone believe him to be the Son of God when they saw his miracles?

Some did; some didn't. Some thought his power came from the evil one. Others were upset that he sometimes worked miracles on the Jewish Sabbath, a day of rest. Reactions were always mixed, as we'll see in the next section.

What kinds of miracles did Jesus work?

There were two main kinds; nature miracle and healing miracles. By nature miracles we mean times where Jesus showed power over nature - when he calmed the storm, or multiplied the loaves and fish, or walked on water. By healing miracles, we mean times when Jesus showed his power over sickness, evil and death - when he cured many people, when he drove out demons, or when he brought people back to life.

Did Jesus ask anything from people before he worked a miracle?

Jesus often looked for faith and trust before he performed a miracle.

For example, a friend of Jesus, called Lazarus, died. By the time Jesus arrived, he had been dead four days. His sisters, Martha and Mary, were weeping.

When Jesus told people to roll away the stone from Lazarus' grave, Martha said that the body would have started to decay. Jesus reminded her: 'Have I not told you that if you believe you will see the glory of God?' (John 11:40). *He then raised Lazarus to life.*

Activities

1. **(a)** How would you react and expect others to react to the following incident?

> Imagine this. You are in a crowd. You see a man in the middle. People want his attention. He calls to someone you know, a friend of yours. Your friend's arm is severely deformed. The man tells your friend to stretch out this arm. Your friend tries. As he does so, the arm becomes completely whole and healthy.

   (b) Suppose someone in the crowd shouted at the man, 'You can't do that, it's against the rules', what would you think?

   (c) Jesus suffered this treatment for healing on the Sabbath. In fact, the Pharisees planned to kill him. What does this tell you about the opposition Jesus faced?

Activities

2. Sometimes Jesus raised dead people back to life. For example, he raised the daughter of Jairus back to life.

   (a) Design the captions to go with the storyboard that show people's faith. Read Mark 5:21-24, 35-43.

   (b) **'Lay your hands on her that she may be saved'** (Jairus to Jesus). Do you think that Jairus had faith in Jesus? Explain why or why not.

   (c) Jairus' faith and trust were tested once again whilst on the way back to his house. How?

   (d) **'Give her something to eat'** (Jesus to Jairus). Jairus' daughter was probably hungry. But can you think of any other reason why Jesus gave this instruction?

Extension

3. We talk about Jairus' daughter or about Lazarus being **raised back to life**. We talk of the **Resurrection** of Jesus. Why is 'resurrection' so different from what happened to Jairus' daughter or to Lazarus?

Glossary Words

mystery   compassion   decay   resurrection

          incarnation   demons   Sabbath

REACTIONS TO JESUS

In John 9, Jesus cured a man who had been blind since birth. This produced a number of different reactions amongst those standing around.

A I don't think the man was really blind from birth

B This Jesus is a sinner. He breaks the Sabbath law

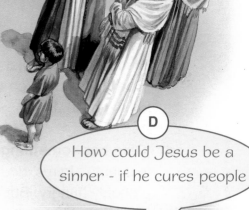

C We are disciples of Moses - not of this man Jesus

D How could Jesus be a sinner - if he cures people

The religious authorities (mainly groups called Scribes and Pharisees) are puzzled. Some think Jesus is a bad man, a sinner. They won't believe his power comes from God. Others can't see how a bad man could do such good things. Many of the ordinary people - including the man who was cured - are happy to become Jesus' followers.

E I believe that Jesus is the Promised One - the Son of God

Activity 4

Study the reactions of the people to the miracles of Jesus. Imagine you are there with them and they ask you what you think. What would you say to each of them?

JESUS WASHES HIS DISCIPLES' FEET

"It was before the festival of the Passover, and Jesus knew that the hour had come for him to pass from this world to the Father. He had always loved those who were his own in the world, but now he showed how perfect his love was.

He came to Simon Peter, who said to him, 'Lord, are you going to wash my feet?' Jesus answered, 'At the moment you do not know what I am doing, but later you will understand'. 'Never!' said Peter, 'You shall never wash my feet'. Jesus replied, 'If I do not wash you, you can have nothing in common with me'.

'Then, Lord,' said Simon Peter 'not only my feet, but my hands and my head as well!' Jesus said, 'No one who has taken a bath needs washing, he is clean all over. You too are clean, though not all of you are.' He knew who was going to betray him, that was why he said, 'though not all of you are'.

When he had washed their feet and put on his outer garment again he went back to the table. 'Do you understand' he said, 'what I have done to you? You call me Master and Lord, and rightly; so I am. If I, then, the Lord and Master, have washed your feet, you should wash each other's feet. I have given you an example so that you may copy what I have done to you." (John 13: 1-15)

St. Paul, in his letter to the Philippians, explains that even though Jesus is God, while he was on earth

"He did not cling to his equality with God, but emptied himself to assume the condition of a slave…"

(Phil. 2: 6-7)

So when Jesus washed the disciples' feet he was not just performing an act of kindness, he was doing the work of a servant.

He did not claim any status for himself or high position of Lord and Master. This is why he said.

"I have given you an example so that you may copy what I have done."

Jesus is not asking us to wash each other's feet, but instead to get out of thinking about our own selfish interests, that is, just thinking about what *we* want. We need to think of the needs of others before our own. This is the message that Jesus has for us.

Judas

It was during the Passover meal, the Last Supper, that Judas left the table and went out to betray Jesus to his enemies, that is, to those who were plotting to arrest him.

Jesus knew that the hour was approaching when his enemies would come, so he tried to both warn and comfort the disciples.

JESUS' FAREWELL TO THE DISCIPLES

This is what Jesus said to his disciples.

"My friends I shall not be with you much longer…" (John 13:33)

"Do not let your hearts be troubled. Trust in God still, and trust in me." (John 14:1)

"I am the Way, the Truth and the Life". (John 14:6)

"If you remain in me and my words remain in you, you may ask what you will and you shall get it." (John 15:7)

"If you keep my commandments you will remain in my love." (John 15:10)

Activities

1. **(a)** Explain in your own words what Jesus wanted the disciples to understand when he washed their feet.

   (b) Give two examples of how we could put others needs before our own.

2. Write a paragraph on what you think were the thoughts going through Jesus' mind when Judas left the table.

3. Choose one of the sayings that Jesus said in his 'farewell' to the disciples. Design a 'Memory Card' with these words, to keep in a place where you will frequently see it.

Research

4. **(a)** Find out what happens in your church on Holy Thursday to remind people of what Jesus did at the Last Supper.

   (b) Start to make a Holy Week booklet so that it will help you and others to understand the things that happen in Holy Week, and to reflect on their meaning.
   (See Teacher's Book, page 71)

   The title of the first section should be **HOLY THURSDAY**.

   Your booklet can include symbols and prayers to meditate with.

Glossary Words

assume	condition	Holy Thursday	betray	Holy Week

BETRAYED BY HIS OWN DISCIPLES

After the Last Supper with his disciples Jesus went to the Garden of Gethsemane with them. It was not long till Judas arrived with guards to have him arrested. They seized Jesus and took him to the high priest's palace. Peter followed and stayed outside the door. The maid on duty at the door said to Peter, '*Aren't you another of that man's disciples?*' He answered, '*I am not*'. Now it was cold and the servants and guards had lit a charcoal fire and were standing there warming themselves; so Peter stood there too, warming himself with the others. (John 18:16-18)

The high priests questioned Jesus but could find no good reason to put him in prison so they sent him to Pilate. By this time one of the high priest's servants said to Peter, '*Didn't I see you in the garden with him*?' Again Peter denied it and at once the cock crew. (John 18:26-27)

Jesus before Pilate

The Jewish authorities led Jesus to Pilate. So Pilate came outside to them and said, '*What charge do you bring against this man?*' They replied, '*If he were not a criminal, we should not be handing him over to you*'. Pilate said, '*Take him yourselves, and try him by your own Law*'. The Jews answered, '*We are not allowed to put a man to death*'. (John 18: 29-32)

Pilate was afraid. He found nothing to accuse Jesus of, and yet he was afraid of the people. Perhaps there would be rioting.

Even though he knew Jesus was innocent, he had him whipped and let the soldiers make cruel fun of him. They even put a crown of thorns on his head. They kept coming up to him and saying, '*Hail king of the Jews!*', and they slapped him in the face.

Pilate thought it might satisfy the crowds once they saw Jesus punished. Yet they shouted all the more: '*Crucify him! Crucify him!*' In the end, Pilate gave in and gave them their wish. (John 19:6)

DISCUSS

Now let us look at some of the different personalities who *were* there, and who helped to crucify Jesus or let Jesus be crucified.

• Those who misunderstood Jesus

Many of the religious experts simply thought Jesus was a threat to the Jewish religion.

They wanted to silence him for good.

Can you think of a situation where people speak the truth and others would rather not listen?

• Those who were easily led

Many of the ordinary people were like this - fickle. They listened to rumour and half-truth. They went with the flow. When a mob shouts, it's easier to shout with them.

Can you think of a situation where people are easily led into doing the wrong thing?

• Those who were too afraid to do the right thing

Pontius Pilate was afraid of the mob and so he let them have their way. The disciples also ran off when things got tough. Only John returned to stand at the cross. Fear drove Peter to deny three times that he even knew Jesus.

Can you think of a situation where people are afraid to do the right thing?

• Those who enjoy picking on weaker people

The Jewish Temple guards and the Roman soldiers found nasty ways to be cruel. Here was a poor man before them, with no-one to speak for him. Maybe they thought he was 'weak'. "We can treat him cruelly and no-one will care."

Can you think of a situation where people are cruel to those who cannot defend themselves?

Activities

1. When Peter heard the 'cock crow' three times he remembered what Jesus had said to him at his farewell.

   Peter wanted to go with Jesus wherever he was going.

   Peter even said:

   'Why can't I follow you now? I will lay down my life for you'. ' Lay down your life for me?' answered Jesus. 'I tell you most solemnly, before the cock crows you will have disowned me three times'.

   (John 13:37-38)

   Now Peter had seen his Lord and Master condemned to death and he had done nothing to help him - Peter told the maidservants that he didn't even know Jesus.

   Write a diary account of what it must have been like for Peter as he reflected on his actions that day.

Thursday	Friday
Morning	Morning
————————	————————
————————	————————
Midday	Midday
————————	————————
————————	————————
Evening	Evening
————————	————————
————————	————————

2. Imagine you are a reporter for the 'Jerusalem Chronicle'.

   Your task is to report on the changing fortunes of this 'Jesus of Nazareth' character.

   # The Jerusalem Chronicle
   ### CHEERS TURN TO JEERS...
   Dramatic downturn for the Nazarene...

   He was welcomed by cheering crowds a week ago. Now, many want him dead.

   In your report, try to find reasons for the change. Include some quotes from the crowds involved.

   ## Research

3. Write an account of what happens in your church on **Good Friday** to put into your Holy Week booklet. Your booklet can include symbols and prayers to meditate on. (See Teacher's Book, page 73)

   ### Glossary Words
   religious experts   verdict

   condemned fair trial

   defendant   Passion Good Friday

Extension

4. A fair trial?

(a) Do you think that Jesus had a fair trial according to our ideas of JUSTICE today? The 'Jesus file' is placed on your desk. You look to see whether the defendant, Jesus of Nazareth, had been given every chance of a fair trial.

(b) Look at the account of the trial (Teacher's Book page 72)

(c) Look at the following questions and write a report.

- Was the defendant found guilty according to the evidence presented?

- Was a verdict already reached before the trial began?

- Was the defendant given a fair chance to defend himself?

- Was the defendant abused in any way?

- Did the judge allow himself to be pressurised in any way?

5. (a) Read slowly the reflection below about the suffering that Jesus went through.

<u>Man of sorrows</u>
He felt the terror and loneliness in the Garden of Gethsemane.
He was arrested at night, after being betrayed by a friend.
He had to suffer the complete desertion of his disciples.
He had to face unjust trials.
He was spat on.
He was beaten and flogged.
He was forced to carry his cross.
He was crucified.
He was buried in a borrowed tomb.

(b) What different types of 'hurt' can you identify in this reflection? Which do you feel is the most hurtful?

(c) Think about the suffering that Mary, his mother, went through. Write another reflection called 'Mother of Sorrows'.

61

RESURRECTION

Jesus' death has its own 'punctuation'. It could be followed with a full stop, a question mark, an exclamation mark, or a 'to be continued' mark.

 Some hoped it would be a full stop. They thought that killing Jesus would be the end of the matter.

 For some, Jesus' death was a question mark. Some of his followers couldn't quite accept that Jesus was finished. Yet, they couldn't understand what could have happened.

 For many of Jesus' followers, his death came as a shocking suprise.

And yet Jesus knew that it was not the end of the story: 'On the third day the Son of Man will rise to life'.

Before Jesus died, he had said to his followers that they would be weeping, but that their sorrow would turn to joy (John 16:20). This is exactly what happened with Mary Magdalene. She wept at the tomb. She didn't recognise Jesus until he called her by name. With joy she ran to tell the others. She was the first witness of the Resurrection of Jesus.

Does it matter whether Jesus rose from the dead or not?

'If Christ has not been raised then our preaching is worthless, and so is your faith.'
St Paul wrote these words to the Christians of Corinth. Does the resurrection matter? It matters enormously. When we as Christians say our hope is in the risen Jesus, we mean it is our **greatest** hope. Without the resurrection all we have is a dead Jesus.

St Paul said that death entered the world because of sin. Death is the 'last enemy' to be defeated. Jesus **beat** death by dying, and by showing us that death **couldn't** keep him. When Jesus rose on the first Easter morning, it was to a brand new kind of life. He promises this same resurrection life to all who hope in him.

Activities

1. Read the speech bubbles below.

A
We had hoped he would be the one who set Israel free. It's now two days since he was killed. We've heard that his tomb is empty.

B
In a short time you will no longer see me, and then a short time later you will see me again.

C
We need to guard the tomb. His disciples might steal the body and claim he has risen from the dead.

D
You are not to suffer and die. Heaven preserve you!

- One was said by the chief priests to Pontius Pilate. (Matthew 27:64)
- One was said by two followers of Jesus on the road to Emmaus. (Luke 24:21)
- One was said by Simon Peter to Jesus (when Jesus said that he was to suffer and die). (Luke 22:33)
- One was said by Jesus himself. (John 16:16)

(a) Fit the speaker with the right speech bubble, A, B, C, or D.

    (i) Which speaker wants to put a **'full stop'** after Jesus' death?

    (ii) Which speaker puts a **'question mark'** after Jesus' death?

    (iii) Which speaker would put an **'exclamation mark'** after Jesus' death?

    (iv) Which speaker puts a **'to be continued'** after Jesus' death?

(b) Create a banner design reflecting your understanding of the resurrection of Jesus and its meaning for us. You can use symbols, colour and images including the punctuation on the previous page.

2. **(a)** Use the idea of 'Reactions' on page 54 to create your own page about the 'Reactions' to the resurrection of Jesus. Use your ICT or drawing skills.

    (b) Why do you think people reacted in different ways to the resurrection?

3. **(a)** Find out what happens in your church on **Holy Saturday** night.

    (b) Complete the section in your Holy Week booklet - use the title **Easter Vigil**. You can use symbols and prayers to meditate on.

5. The Work of the Apostles

Know and reflect on our calling to be disciples of Jesus

WHAT IS A DISCIPLE?

Disciple simply means 'follower' or 'learner'. You have been a disciple all your life. You followed and learnt from parents, aunts, uncles and other  relatives. When very small, you tried to copy those around you. You were a learner. You were learning to develop as a human being. What did you learn? How did you learn to speak, act and think?

Now, you might be a 'disciple' of someone else, for example, bands, sports stars, TV personalities. You might like what these people do and in some way try to be like them. You might stick their names and pictures on your walls or in your diary. Why do you choose these people? You think they're good, interesting, exciting. The trouble is you probably don't really *know* whether they're good in other ways or not.

As Christians we believe that Jesus is the Way, the Truth and the Life. He is good in every way. He will teach us to be fully human, fully alive.

Jesus will show us the secret of what is really and truly important in life.

THE INVITATION TO BE A DISCIPLE

For many Christians the invitation card arrives early - even before they can read it.

It arrives when they're baptised. Later, when they are confirmed they pick up and read the invitation card for themselves. Others are invited too. What is this invitation all about? What's inside the envelope? Would you open it?

A Personal Invitation

R.S.V.P

THE INVITATION

At Baptism we are each invited to be a disciple. It is a bit like receiving an invitation card with the instructions about what we must do in order to take part. With this invitation come the gifts we need in order to accept it. As we grow older and prepare for the Sacrament of Confirmation, we must consider the invitation for ourselves and what it is that Jesus is asking of us.

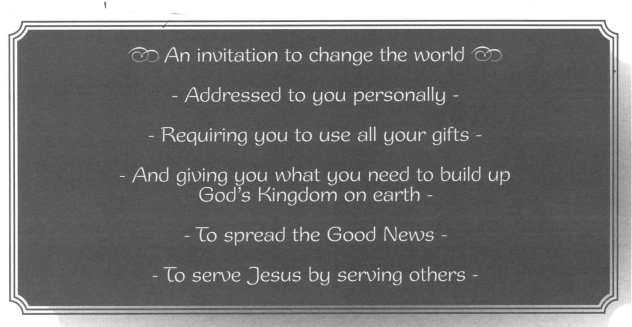

∞ An invitation to change the world ∞

- Addressed to you personally -

- Requiring you to use all your gifts -

- And giving you what you need to build up God's Kingdom on earth -

- To spread the Good News -

- To serve Jesus by serving others -

Activities

1. Take a few minutes to be very still while the invitation above is read.

2. (a) Think about a person you admire.

   (b) What is it about this person you would want to imitate? Why?

   (c) Are there any qualities you would not want to imitate? Why?

3. On an A4 sheet of paper draw or stick a picture of Jesus at the top and you in the middle. Put 'thought bubbles' around your picture and write in them what you can do to imitate Jesus.

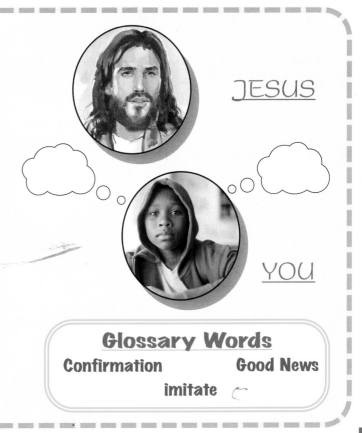

JESUS

YOU

Glossary Words

Confirmation   Good News

imitate

THE CALL OF THE DISCIPLES

Imagine this. A stranger walks into a mechanics' yard. Everyone's busy, hard at work trying to earn the little that they live on. He sees two mechanics and walks over to them. He says to them, 'Follow me, and I will teach you to fix the world.'

The mechanics then drop their tools and go with the stranger. The stranger walks on and says follow me to the two other mechanics working hard. Their father owns the mechanics' yard. 'Follow me,' he says to them.

What are they thinking? What would you be thinking? Is this stranger mad? But they get up, leave everything behind - their father, their business - and follow him. Are they mad too?

Now listen to this passage from St Mark's Gospel.

As Jesus walked along the shore of Lake Galilee, he saw two fishermen, Simon and his brother Andrew, bringing fish with a net. Jesus said to them, 'Come with me, and I will teach you to draw people to me.' At once they left their nets and went with him. He went a little farther on and saw two other brothers, James and John, the sons of Zebedee. They were in their boat getting their nets ready. As soon as Jesus saw them, he called them; they left their father Zebedee in the boat with the hired men and went with Jesus.

What was in their minds? Why did they go? Did they know Jesus? St Luke tells us that the fishermen had spent the night fishing without any success. Then Jesus helped them make a great catch. After this they went with him. They left behind their old lives forever.

Matthew (or Levi) had not lived a very good life. He was a tax collector - someone hated by ordinary Jews because he demanded too much money from them to make his living. He was chosen to be one of Jesus' closest followers. Mary Magdalene proved to be one of the most faithful disciples of Jesus, and yet she hadn't led a very good life before.

The first disciples Jesus chose were not exactly religious experts themselves. They were ordinary working people. Not one of them could be called a student, a scholar, a professor, a priest, or a prophet. They'd be lucky to have the basics of reading and a little writing.

Simon Peter was a married man who became a full-time helper of Jesus. Somehow, things worked out for him and his family. Besides, most of the followers of Jesus weren't asked to follow him everywhere he went. They could be faithful disciples whilst staying in their own towns and villages.

What Jesus asks

If Jesus had made an advertisement for disciples, he'd have put on the details: 'No experience necessary' and 'No previous qualifications needed'. He would train them from scratch. So he didn't mind what they had done or been in the past; he only wanted them to be ready. Ready to do what?

What did he ask of his disciples? Three things to start with: he wanted them to:

Turn, Drop and Trust.

'**Turn**' - means repent, turn away from sin and towards God.

'**Drop**' - means put aside anything that stops you receiving his invitation. If you're too attached to your job and your money then you can't open your arms to receive what he has to give.

'**Trust**' - means being open and honest like a very young child.
Jesus wasn't asking his followers to quarrel and steal each other's toys; he was asking them to copy small children in the way they trust, are joyful, laugh and are open and honest. Later on, Jesus would ask more of his followers. He said that they must be prepared to '*take up their cross*' - to face tough times for Jesus' sake and for the sake of his message.

Activities

1. Think of three questions you would ask Jesus about being a disciple if he visited your classroom.

2. Imagine this is a live phone-in programme. **Jason**, **Sabina** and **Romero** phone in. Here is what they say.

But I've not lived a very good life up to now. I can't possibly be a follower of Jesus.

But I'm married and I've got a family to look after. I can't possibly think about being a full-time disciple.

But I don't know too much about religion - I'm not an expert in religious matters.

Jason

Sabina

Romero

Draw the programme presenter's speech bubbles to show how you think he replied.

3. Use **Turn**, **Drop** and **Trust** as the basis for dance or mime to express your understanding of the meaning of discipleship.

4. **(a)** Read the story of St. Gabriel Possenti (Teacher's Book page 76-77)

   (b) In what way did Gabriel **Turn**, **Drop** and **Trust**?

5. **(a)** Read the story of St. Ignatius Loyola (Teacher's Book page 78)

   (b) Design a story board to show the point of **Turn**, **Drop** and **Trust** in the life of Ignatius.

Glossary Words

prophet   repent   attached   discipleship

DEATH, RESURRECTION AND ASCENSION

They deserved to be sacked: the lot of them. Judas betrayed Jesus with a kiss; Peter betrayed him with his lies; the rest betrayed him by running off when he was arrested. Only John came back to stand by the cross as Jesus died. And when the news came of his resurrection, they wouldn't believe it…

So when Jesus rose from death and returned to the disciples, they should have been fired and forgotten. So what did happen to them?

▶ Jesus was disappointed in them. Not for abandoning him, but for refusing to believe he had risen.

▶ Jesus blessed them. 'Peace be with you,' he said to them.

▶ Jesus gave them some instructions. 'Go out and make disciples of all nations. Wait for the power from on high to come down on you.'

▶ Jesus made them promises. 'I will be with you until the end of time.' He promised to send them the gift of the Holy Spirit.

▶ Then he was taken up to heaven out of their sight.

▶ The disciples who were very close to Jesus and chosen by him became known as Apostles.

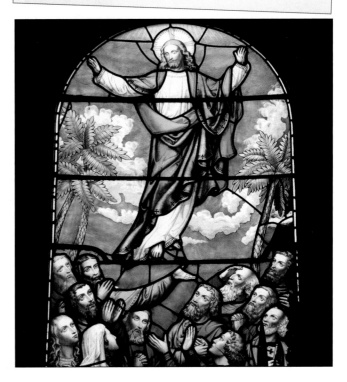

When God chooses people he does not always choose the good, the great and the best. He chooses people who are imperfect, and by his grace and power he changes them.

Jesus knew the disciples' weaknesses but he also knew that his power and grace could transform their weaknesses into strength.

Activities

1. **(a)** Think about how people are chosen to be in a team or to do a job.

Choose one example and give some reasons why a person might be chosen.

(b) Read about these disciples who became great men for God. Find and list some of their weaknesses.

St Thomas

St Peter

St James

St John

Some clues: John 20:24-25;
Matthew 26:69-75 & Mark 10:35-39

(c) Now find out how Jesus responded to either Thomas or Peter.

(Clues John 20: 26-29; John 21:15-17)

2. Work in Groups: Imagine you have been invited to draw up plans for a CD-ROM on some of the Twelve Apostles.

Each person in your group chooses one of the apostles to write an outline of the most interesting things in his life.

(a) This week start by choosing an apostle and introducing him to your readers.

(b) Draw up a plan of what you would like to be able to find out about him.

(c) In groups discuss ideas for the CD-ROM.

- Where could you find more information?

- Where could you find pictures?

- Think about the CD-ROMs that you enjoy using: what makes them good fun to use?

- What ideas could you use for this CD-ROM to make it enjoyable for others?
  Try: www.ainglkiss.com/apo/ for background information.
  Try: www.tere.org ICT in RE (Thomas).

Glossary Words

'power on high'   apostles

imperfect   grace   transform

THE HOLY SPIRIT

Jesus had promised the Apostles that he would not leave them orphans but he would send the Holy Spirit who would teach them all things. (John 16:13)

This poem describes the transforming power of the Holy Spirit on the Apostles.

> ### ∼ The Holy Spirit ∼
>
> There is a power of fire and flame
> the Holy Spirit is its name.
> It brings us peace; it brings us love;
> a gust of wind, a pure white dove.
>
> When the disciples' hope seemed lost
> the Spirit came at Pentecost.
> It changed their lives, and made them feel
> that Jesus lived. His word was real.
>
> Oh, the excitement of that day
> when fears and doubts were swept away.
> With pounding hearts and racing feet
> they spoke to the people in the street.
>
> And as they spoke the truth was clear,
> the Spirit drew God's people near.
> They longed for God with a new desire
> when the Spirit came as flames of fire.
>
> (© Susannah White)

We believe that the Holy Spirit transformed the Apostles as they patiently waited in the Upper Room in Jerusalem.

Read the story of how it happened.

When Pentecost day came round, they had all met in one room, when suddenly they heard what sounded like a powerful wind from heaven, the noise of which filled the entire house in which they were sitting; and something appeared to them that seemed like tongues of fire; these separated and came to rest on the head of each of them. They were all filled with the Holy Spirit, and began to speak foreign languages as the Spirit gave them all the gift of speech. (Acts 2:1-4)

BEFORE

Disciple betrays leader with a kiss
and gets 30 coins for it....

**DISCIPLES REFUSE TO BELIEVE
'RISEN AGAIN' RUMOURS**
- WOMAN TOLD TO STOP DREAMING -

The Rock's Shattering Denial
Servant woman speaks out...

References for evidence - Matthew 26:47-50
& Matthew 27:3-4; Matthew 26:29-75;
See *www.tere.org* 'Support Material' for texts.

AFTER

**Followers of Nazarene Dazzle
Pentecost Crowds**
Everyone understood, says witness...

Drunk on Wine at Nine?
Sect leaders are drunkards,
say some...

**3000 JOIN NEW SECT AFTER
PREACHING OF GALILEANS**
CRUCIFIED LEADER HAS RISEN, SAY FOLLOWERS

Mark 14:66-74; Luke 22:55-62; Mk16: 11-12;
Acts 2:5-7; Acts 2:12-13; Acts 2:41-42.

Activities

1. Study the picture of the Holy Spirit descending on the Apostles on the previous page.

   (a) What symbols do you see in this picture? (Symbols can include shapes, objects, colours and gestures).

   (b) Why do you think the artist included them?

   (c) Why do you think the artist put Mary in the middle of the picture?

2. The 'headlines' above are all about the disciples and their time with Jesus.

Pick **one** headline from the **'Before'** and one from the **'After'** section and tell the story behind them. See references above for help.

3. Write a poem or tell a story entitled 'The Transforming Spirit'.

   • You might like to use some of the ideas from the poem 'The Holy Spirit'.

   • You need to show how the first followers of Jesus were changed by the Spirit.

   • You should try to show how the same Spirit can transform lives today.

Glossary Words

orphan   Pentecost   Upper Room
     sect   Nazarene

RESULTS OF THE TRANSFORMATION

The coming of the Holy Spirit made all the difference to the first followers of Jesus.

> ▸ They were completely united as a group.
>
> ▸ Their preaching touched the hearts of many who heard them.
>
> ▸ There were miraculous signs that showed their message was from God.
>
> ▸ There was new opposition from those who didn't wish the Gospel to spread.

Fruits of the Holy Spirit

The Holy Spirit brings **love, joy, peace, patience, kindness, goodness, trustfulness, gentleness and self-control**. Because of the Holy Spirit people of many languages came together and understood the apostles very well.

New people brought into the Church

On the first day, as a result of Peter's preaching, three thousand people came to believe in Jesus. The 'fire of the Spirit' was in Peter's words. Many more people joined them in the Church.

As the centuries went by, more and more people became Christians.

There are now many millions all over the face of the earth. But it is the same Spirit and the same Baptism that every Christian receives, from Pentecost to the present day.

Miraculous Signs

The miraculous signs that God worked through Peter and Paul and other apostles impressed many of these early believers. In this way, God showed that their preaching was true.

Activities

1. Read the story of the early Christian community (Acts 2:42-47).

   (a) Then copy and complete the table below.

United in belief	They remained faithful to the teaching of the apostles
United in worship	
United in goodness	
United in joy	

   (b) In this story there is only one broken thing - what?
   Why was that important?

2. Imagine you have found a Bible with Acts 2:42-47 missing.
   www.tere.org 'Support Material'.

   (a) Why do you think it would be important to find that missing page?

   (b) What can we learn from the example of the early Church?

3. **(a)** Read about the cure of the man who could not walk (Acts 3:1-10).

   Bible or see *www.tere.org* (Support material for scripture texts).

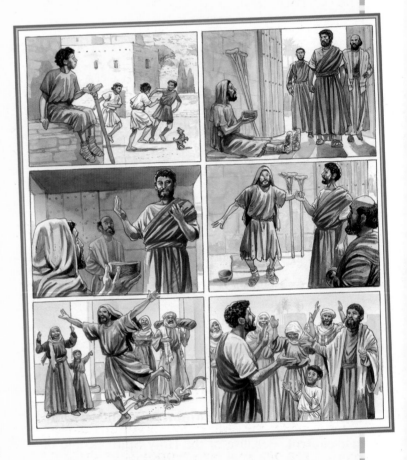

   (b) Design the script for the six pictures of the storyboard that will communicate what is important about this story. Use the account from Acts 3:1-10 to help you.

   (c) Who cured the man (read carefully!)?

NEW OPPOSITION

The message that the followers of Jesus were preaching was very powerful and people were eager to listen. Many of the religious authorities in Jerusalem were suspicious of the early Church. They debated amongst themselves. Was this the work of God or of human imagination?

Gamaliel, a wise and respected Pharisee spoke up and warned them against persecuting the members of the Church because it might be like trying to fight with God…

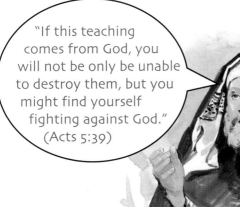

"If this teaching comes from God, you will not be only be unable to destroy them, but you might find yourself fighting against God." (Acts 5:39)

After a while, the authorities forgot this advice. Saul, a zealous Jew, was working for the total destruction of the Church. Stephen, a Christian deacon, had been stoned to death as Saul watched. James, the fisherman, called along with his brother John to be an Apostle, was beheaded by Herod. Simon Peter and his companions had been arrested at least twice, flogged once and warned to stop preaching. They would not stop. King Herod, the murderer of James, decided to have Peter imprisoned under heavy guard.

If the ringleader was silenced, maybe the others would give up too. Not so! The Apostles believed that if God was on their side, no power on earth will keep them quiet.

Activities

1. **A miraculous escape…**
    Read the story of Peter's escape in Acts 12:1-19.

    (a) You are a detective in Herod's police. You are sent to investigate this mysterious escape.
    You interview:

    - the maker of the double chains that fastened Peter;

    - the two guards between whom Peter was sleeping;

    - the other guards;

    - the maker of the iron gate leading to the city.

    (b) Imagine the answers these people gave, and write a report to King Herod. Start it like this:
    'To your highness, Herod Agrippa, King of Judaea and Samaria…

Glossary Words

Opposition	zealous	deacon
	Judaea	Samaria

RESURRECTION - KEYSTONE AND STUMBLING BLOCK

Every apostle preached about Jesus having risen from the dead. Whenever you read of Peter and Paul preaching about Jesus, the 'sticking point' for the people listening, is often when they speak of Jesus' resurrection. It is the 'keystone' - the most important part of their message. It is also a 'stumbling block' (something that causes a problem), because some people could not bring themselves to believe it.

The apostles preached the resurrection of Jesus and their teaching is very important in the lives of all Christians today.

▶ It gives HOPE that death is not the end.

▶ Death was NOT the END for Jesus and it is NOT the END for us.

▶ Jesus' resurrection broke the power of sin and this gives us HOPE because we know that GOOD will triumph.

St. Paul tells us that we have every reason to hope: "With God on our side who can be against us?"

> God freely gave up his own Son for our benefit... Jesus not only died for us - he rose from the dead, and there at God's right hand he stands and pleads for us.

> Nothing therefore can come between us and the love of Jesus, even if we are troubled or worried, or being persecuted, or lacking food or clothes, or being threatened or even attacked. Through all these sufferings we will triumph through the power of Jesus.
>
> (Rom. 8: 31-37 adapted)

When people asked Paul questions about the resurrection, he did not explain in detail but said that we will all be changed. It will happen 'in the twinkling of an eye, when the last trumpet sounds!'
(1 Cor. 15:51-52)

Activities

1. What reply did Peter give to the person who asked if he could be saved? (Acts 2:38-39)

2. Look at the picture on page 76. Imagine you are there with all the people. What questions would you like to ask?

3. Listen to 'And the Trumpet shall Sound' from Handel's *Messiah* (Pt. 2) based on 1 Cor. 15: 51-52. In what way does this music express the Christian hope of the Resurrection?

4. Now read on from the story of Pentecost (Acts 2:1-41) (Teacher's Book page 78).

    (a) Imagine you are Peter and you want your message to reach everyone everywhere.

    -   You are able to use modern means of communication.

    -   You can prepare a speech or write an article.

    -   You could write a rap or lyric to a song.

    -   Remember you want everybody to repent and be baptised.

Glossary Words
gentile

6. Called to Serve

> *Be aware of Jesus' teaching and example of service and how we should try to be like him*

SERVICE IN WORD AND DEED

- Jesus came to bring us the fullness of life:

- He came to show us by his own actions how we should love one another.

- We are all called to love one another by the way we live our lives.

Here are some of the ways Jesus showed his love for us.

Jesus had time for 'bad people' - like sinners

Jesus had time for 'little people' - like children

God became one of us in Jesus

Jesus showed us how to serve. At the Last Supper he washed the disciples' feet

Jesus had time for sick people - he cured them

Jesus teaches us that whatever we do to help those in need, we do to him. He has promised that the day will come when he will say to those people who help others:

> "Come you that are blessed by my Father! I was hungry and you fed me, thirsty and you gave me a drink; I was a stranger and you received me in your homes, naked and you clothed me; I was sick and you took care of me; in prison and you visited me." (Matthew 25:14-23)

CALLED TO SERVE

There is no one on this earth like you. What you are and what you have are unique. Only you can take the part that is meant for you.

Reflection

God has created me to do Him some service;
He has committed some work to me which He has not committed to another.
I have my mission...
I am a link in a chain,
a bond of connection between persons...
I shall do good,
I shall do His work.
Therefore, I will trust Him.
Whatever, wherever I am,
I cannot be thrown away.

(From Cardinal Newman's Reflection)

Activities

1. **Only you will do...**
   In the *Lord of the Rings*, Frodo Baggins has a mission in life.

This mission can only be carried out by him, and he must choose whether to accept it or not.

As Christians, we believe that we, too, have a mission in life, something that only each one of us can offer back to God.

Design an acrostic with the word 'UNIQUE'.

Unlike any other
New path for me
I
Q
U
E

Try to get across:
- that there is no one like you;
- that you have a special mission in life.

2. Some of the things Jesus said to the disciples are listed here, from St. Mark's Gospel.

Stay with me (14:32)

Be on your guard (13:33)

Go out to the whole world and proclaim the Gospel (16:16)

Take up your cross (8:34)

Forget self (8:34)

Come away with me to some lonely place (6:13)

Follow me (1:17)

(a) Choose any three sayings. After reading them, try to explain how the first disciples might have put these words into action.

(b) Try to explain how a Christian today might put these words into action.

3. Think about some of the examples of service that Jesus gave us.
   (a) Which example best helps you to understand how Jesus served others? Explain.

   (b) There is one enormous example of how Jesus served us that is missing from the box. What is it?

4. **ASPECTS OF LOVE**
   (a) There are three aspects of LOVE: CHOOSING, FEELING and ACTING. Look at the following situations and say which aspect of love is shown in each example.

   A - Laximi and her son, Vikram (3), go shopping in a supermarket. Vikram grabs a bag of sweets. Laximi refuses to let her son have the sweets, no matter how loudly he squeals.

   B - A new girl has arrived in Form 6C, and Andrew realises she is lonely. The class teacher asks for someone to volunteer to be with the new girl for the school day and help her settle in. Andrew is first to volunteer.

   C - Two children, John and Liz, go shopping. They have only a few minutes to buy sweets when suddenly they see an old lady fall and decide to help her.

   (b) Read the three situations again. Are any of them examples of service? Give reasons for your answer.

   Glossary Words
   unique   mission
          service

WHO AM I?

We don't know how old the universe is. The latest guess is around 15 billion years. Human beings have been around for very little of that time. If the universe were a day old, humans would have spent about half a second in it.

Yet before the world was created, God had you in mind - **you**, reading this page right now. God planted in you special talents, gifts and possibilities. You are part of God's plan. You are invited to serve.

Reflection

You are very special.
In all the world there is nobody
like you.
Since the beginning of the world there
has never been another person
like you.
Nobody has your smile, your eyes,
your hands, your hair.
Nobody owns your handwriting,
your voice.
You're special.

Nobody can paint your brush strokes.
Nobody has your taste for food
or music or dance or art.
Nobody in the universe sees
things as you do.
In all time there has never been
anyone who laughs exactly in
your way.
And what makes you laugh or cry or
think may have a totally different
response in another.
So, you're special.

Talents

Are you as talented as this boxer? Are you lightning fast? Strong? Quick on your feet? Do you have a lot of energy? Are you world class? Perhaps you don't have these talents. But you have other talents, maybe much greater than these.

This boxer got badly hurt and nearly died. He was severely brain damaged. He spent months in intensive care. He could hardly move. Then, little by little he tried to walk again. After more painful months he just began to take a few steps. Then he entered the London Marathon. It took him six days.

Even when his boxing talents were taken from him, he still had some awesome gifts: to fight for his life; to have courage, patience and hope to walk again; to have generosity to help others worse off then he was. So you must never, never say that you have nothing to offer!

Using your talents - some mistakes...

Mistake 1: *"I've got nothing to offer compared to others"*

This was made by the third servant in the Parable of the Talents. (Read the Parable in St Matthew's Gospel, 25:14-30). He buried what he had been given and then gave it back to his master. He took no risks. His master was furious, and threw this servant out.

Lesson 1: *Take a risk.*

Mistake 3: *"I'm so gifted and strong that I don't need God's help"*

This was Simon Peter's mistake. When Jesus told the disciples that they would all run away when trouble came to him, Peter said that he would never run away, even if all the others did. Peter was relying on his own strength. It was a bad mistake. He ended up denying three times that he even knew Jesus.

Lesson 3: *Rely on God.*

Mistake 2: *"I use my talents - but only for myself"*

Many people think that Jesus' message is 'use your talents'. It is not. Jesus' message is 'use your talents for my Kingdom'. A robber 'uses' his talents to trick and force others to give him money. He also takes risks. Jesus wants his followers to use their talents - but for the building up of his Kingdom.

Lesson 2: *Serve God's Kingdom.*

Mistake 4: *"I'll wait for the 'big' moment to show my talents"*

Many people think that God wants them to do extraordinary things. They don't realise that God wants them to do ordinary things extraordinarily well. Jesus said that the person who was faithful in little things could be trusted with great responsibility. What did he mean? He meant that if you don't use your talents faithfully in the ordinary things of life, you won't be ready for the 'big' moments in life which also demand your talents.

Lesson 4: *Serve God in the daily routine of life.*

In summary

Do not waste time: try to use your talents, whilst depending on God to bring success. Use your talents for the service of God's Kingdom, and don't forget that this service is required in the ordinary, day-to-day life. The Church, the Family of God, is a community of talented people, all with the purpose of increasing the knowledge and love of Jesus Christ in the world around us. Jesus wishes to use all his followers and all their talents to reach others who have never experienced his love.

Activities

1. **(a)** As a class, try to think of obvious and hidden talents.

   (b) Add these to a table your teacher will make.

   (c) Which talents are more important? Give reasons for your answer.

   (d) Why do we all have different talents?

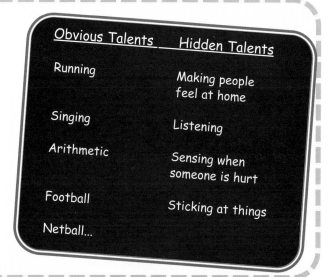

Obvious Talents | Hidden Talents

Running

Singing

Arithmetic

Football

Netball...

Making people feel at home

Listening

Sensing when someone is hurt

Sticking at things

2. Fit the parts of sentences together in the right order.

A talent is a -	a talent for imagination, poetry, mathematics, and so on.
Some talents may be physical -	a talent for friendship, for bringing out the best in others, for listening, and so on.
Some talents may be social -	gift or ability that we have been given.
Some talents may be mental -	a talent for swimming, running, dancing, and so on.

3. **(a)** Think of the talents your friend has. Try to list **three** talents that they would say they have. Try to list three talents that you see in them, talents which may not be obvious to them. Copy and complete the table.

Talents my friend would say they have	Talents I see in my friend

   (b) A friend says to you that they have no talents, that they are useless. Think of two pieces of advice you might give them to help them discover their talents.

4. (a) Read the eco fable below.

Eco Fable

Elzeard Bouffier was a shepherd who had retired into a deforested area in the south of France after he had lost his family. Between 1910 and 1947, completely on his own and without help, he planted hundreds of thousands of acorns in devastated places. Over the decades so much water was stored by the young trees that grew from those seeds, that the streams ran again in the dried brook beds. When Elzeard Bouffier died at the age of 87, happy after almost forty years of his life's work, the deforested region where he had planted the acorns was once again beautiful forest for people and animals.

(b) How was it that one person, all on his own, was able to make such a difference?

5. (a) Read the story of the Emperor of China.

The Emperor of China

The Emperor of China was getting old. He gathered together one hundred young people from all over his empire, people who were talented. He gave each a seed, telling them, 'Plant the seed, and after one year return to me with the results. When I see the results of your planting, one of you shall then be named as emperor after me.' A year later, the hundred returned to the emperor's court. His gaze fell on the only pot where there was no plant. The seed buried in it had not germinated. It belonged to a young man named Deng. The emperor stopped in front of him and said, 'You, Deng, shall be my successor.'

5. (b) Can you guess why Deng was made the next emperor?
Your teacher will tell you the answer if you can't guess.

(c) When you know the answer, what message of Jesus does the whole story show?

Research

6. (a) Plan an assembly on 'Small things make a big difference'.

Here are some ideas to use:

- A small power failure in Ohio shut down the electricity across North East America.

- A tiny break in a circuit board can shut down a computer server.

- One smile on a miserable day, can make you feel better about the world.

- A tiny spark can start a forest fire.

- One small piece of computer language (a virus) can create a terrible mess.

- One tiny candle flame can light up a great dark space.

(b) Our gifts and talents however small can make a great difference.

Create a classroom display on how doing small things with great love can make a difference.

SACRAMENT OF CONFIRMATION

Confirmation is one of the seven sacraments of the Church. Sacraments are the ways God has chosen to give us a share in his own life. In the Sacrament of Baptism we became members of the Church, through the Sacrament of Confirmation we share fully in the Church's mission.

Confirmation completes our Baptism in two ways:
• We receive the gifts of the Holy Spirit;
• We affirm the promises made at our Baptism.

In Confirmation we are given gifts, which are not just for ourselves, but for others. We are called by God to live more like Jesus and to share in the work of Jesus today in our world. We were first called to this in Baptism. Through the Sacraments of Baptism, Eucharist, Reconciliation and Confirmation we are given all the strength and all the gifts necessary to do what God asks of us.

During the Sacrament of Confirmation, the Bishop stretches out his hands and calls down God's Spirit upon those to be confirmed. The Holy Spirit is the Gift that contains all gifts.

Confirmation is a call from God to share in the work of Jesus. This call from God is called a vocation and the work we are asked to do is our mission.

GIFTS OF THE HOLY SPIRIT

When a person is being confirmed the Bishop prays for the gifts of the Holy Spirit for those to be confirmed.

These gifts are given to you to enable you to be a committed Christian. They build on the natural talents and gifts that you already have.

There are two stained-glass windows in the pictures. They have similar colours in them. In one the light is flooding through; in the other, it is not. The Holy Spirit is like the light that makes your 'true colours' (your talents and gifts) shine out.

Wisdom

- To have wisdom is to see things as God sees them. It helps us to be truly wise and to follow the way of God.

Understanding

- This is the gift that helps us to understand all that Jesus has told us.

Right Judgement

- This gift will help us to know what is right and what is wrong when faced with difficult situations.

Knowledge

- This gift helps us to recognise the goodness and greatness of God and to see the world as it really is.

Courage

- To have courage is to do the right thing even when you're afraid. Or it's to keep doing the right thing even when you're bored or discouraged. Physical courage is risking your own safety for what is right. Moral courage is risking your relationship with others for what is right. The two kinds of courage go hand in hand.

Wonder and Awe

- The gift of wonder and awe means that:

• God is infinite and infinitely mysterious.

• This infinite God loves each one of us.

• God's creation is beautiful and inspiring.

Reverence

- This gift helps us to love God and each other.

Activities

Imagine the following situations:

1. Suppose Tom's lottery ticket had the numbers to win a million - and he didn't bother to check. He threw the ticket into the fire. Later, he finds out he had the winning numbers... Tom is obviously upset. In fact, he's so down and depressed that he thinks he'll never be happy again. Is Tom **wise** to think in this way? Why or why not?

2. Robert threatens to hit Sam if he doesn't give him his dinner money. Sam refuses to give him the money.

   (a) What kind of **courage** is Sam showing?

   (b) Robert is a friend of yours and you tell him he's wrong to steal dinner money from others. What kind of **courage** are you showing?

3. Think of an example to explain the gift of **knowledge**.

4. An astronaut described what it was like to look back at the earth as he travelled farther and farther away from it.

'The Earth reminded us of a Christmas tree ornament hanging in the blackness of space. As we got farther and farther away it diminished in size. Finally it shrank to the size of a marble, the most beautiful marble you can imagine. That beautiful, warm, living object looked so fragile, so delicate, that if you touched it with a finger it would crumble and fall apart. Seeing this has to change a man, has to make a man appreciate the creation of God and the love of God.'

Which gift of the Holy Spirit was he using?

5. Imagine you are in a country where Christians are forbidden to practise their faith.

   • You have been hired to watch someone suspected of being a Christian.

   • You are to collect evidence to prove that this is true.

   • What sort of evidence would you look for?

Glossary Words

mysterious   infinite

MANY WAYS TO SERVE

The Sacrament of Confirmation enables us to serve God more fully in the world.

We serve God in a variety of ways:

- in our relationships;
- in our work;
- in our leisure;
- in our service to others.

Some serve God by taking **religious vows** and becoming a religious brother or sister.

Some serve God in **Holy Orders**, as a deacon, priest or bishop.

Mary served Jesus all her life. Mary was married to Joseph.

Paul served God by preaching and writing.

Martha and Mary served by their hospitality and friendship.

GOD CALLS

We are **all** called to use our talents for the good of others. Here is an example of what some **young people** did: It was Christmas time. Giving and receiving presents was part of the celebration. News reports showed the terrible conditions of orphan children in some countries. School children packed shoe boxes with all sorts of things like little toys, coloured pencils, chocolate, soap, and other small gifts. These were all collected and taken to children in orphanages in Eastern Europe.

ANNALENA TONELLI

Annalena Tonelli is an example of someone who dedicated her whole life to serving others.

"When I was a little girl I decided to be for other people - the poor, the suffering, the abandoned, the unloved - and this is what I have been and will continue to be until the end of my life. I wanted to follow only Jesus Christ. Nothing else interested me so strongly: he and the poor in him." In an ordinary way Annalena's life was extraordinary.

In October 2003 Annalena was murdered in Africa.

SISTER JOAN O'CALLAGHAN

Sr. Joan believed that her mission was to help the poor in the shanty town of El Salvador in Peru.

She spent many years feeding the hungry and teaching the people about the life of Jesus. She gave the people a great love for the Bible and they continue to tell others how the 'Word of God' changed their lives.

A VARIETY OF VOCATIONS TOGETHER

In the Church today there is a great variety of organisations where lay people and religious work together to promote justice, peace and harmony in the world.

For example, Pax Christi is an international organisation. Most of its members are lay people. Their aim is to search for ways to:-

violence ends where love begins

- Challenge those who often use the path of violence as a means of solving problems.

- Challenge a world which accepts that it is legal to produce and sell weapons of death.

- Say 'NO' to policies that promote the use of violence.

- Say 'NO' to the production and selling of arms in the world.

Members of PAX CHRISITI believe life is sacred; they want to do something to protect and celebrate life.

Activities

1. **(a)** Read or listen to the story of the life of Annalena Tonelli.
(Teacher's Book page 83)

(b) Look back to the 'Reflection' on page 81.

In what ways do you think Annalena responded to God's call to serve? Try to think of at least three ways.

(c) Do you think her story will be an inspiration to others?
Why or why not?

2. **(a)** Read or listen to the story of Sr. Joan. (Teacher's Book page 84)

(b) In what way do you think her work was inspired by the gifts of the Holy Spirit?

(c) Name the gifts she used most and explain how she used them.

3. **(a)** In groups of six prepare for an imaginary TV Chat Show: 'Called to Serve'

PART - 1
Each person chooses to be one of the following:

• Nurse

• Factory worker

• Farmer

• Parent

• Lay-missionary - Annalena
(Read story to help you prepare)

• Religious Sister- Sr. Joan
(Read story to help you prepare)

Write down what you think are the 'JOYS' and 'CHALLENGES' of your imaginary vocation - you can get help from others in your group.

PART - 2
Your teacher picks one vocation out of a box and selects a group to provide a person with that imaginary vocation. The pupil takes the 'HOT SEAT' and all the other groups ask him or her questions about the 'Joys' and 'Challenges' of that vocation.

Glossary Words

ophanage	priest	vocation	harmony
Leisure	religious	shanty town	bishop

SACRAMENT OF MARRIAGE

Marriage is one of the seven sacraments of the Catholic Church. When a couple marry, they make vows before God and the Church.

Through this outward sign, God gives inward grace to the couple. This grace unites them as husband and wife. It also prepares them for their married life together.

Marriage is a little bit like bridges. Bridges are beautiful, but they need a lot of work. There are some old bridges that have to be painted from one end to the other. Once that's finished, the workers start again. Marriage is beautiful. It is a special way to serve God. But it's a life's work. The bond of marriage is like a bridge that always needs looking after.

Many Christians today are **married**. They serve God by loving their husband or wife and by bringing up their children well. Married Christians serve the Kingdom of God and help to build it up.

- Marriage is part of God's plan for man and woman.

- God joins a man and woman in marriage and blesses their life together.

- The love they have for one another is a little mirror of the love Jesus has for his Church.

- Their love is faithful love and lasts until death.

- Their love is more than just feeling, it is rooted in commitment and service.

- The Christian married couple should wish to become parents and accept children lovingly from God.

- They are meant to bring their children up well and help them understand the Christian faith.

SACRAMENT OF HOLY ORDERS

Look at this picture. It is of a man who is being ordained (made) a priest. Like marriage, this is also a sacrament. It is the sacrament of Holy Orders or Ordination. As in marriage, God acts through outward signs to pour grace into the soul.

When a priest is ordained he is able to celebrate Mass. This is a very great privilege because the Mass makes present the mystery of Jesus' death on the cross and his rising from the dead.

Priests are like shepherds to God's people, the Church. A good shepherd looks after his flock, feeding them, guiding them and looking after them in times of need. A priest, too, nourishes God's people with God's Word and the Holy Eucharist.

A priest guides the people by helping them understand what Jesus wants. He looks after the people by visiting the sick, comforting those who are heartbroken and offering Jesus' forgiveness in the Sacrament of Reconciliation.

Activities

1. In what ways could a married couple help to build up the Kingdom of God?

2. **(a)** The wedding vows are written below. Can you guess which words fit the gaps (numbered 1-6)?

    (b) Take one phrase from the vows and write what you think it means.

    > I (name) do take thee (name) to be my lawful wedded wife/husband, to ___1___ and to hold from this day forward, for better for ___2___, for richer for ___3___, in ___4___ and in health, to ____5___ and to cherish, till ___6___ do us part.

    (c) Imagine you had to design a symbol to sum up the meaning of these vows. What symbol would you design and why?

3. Remind yourself of the work of a shepherd. Why are priests sometimes thought of as 'shepherds' to God's people, the Church? Give three reasons.

Glossary Words

cherish	bond	Reconciliation
vows	outward sign	inward grace	Eucharist

GLOSSARY

Absolute - Complete

Adoration - Worship

Adultery - When a husband or wife is unfaithful to their marriage promises

Altar - The table on which the priest celebrates Mass

Apostles - The twelve disciples who were closest to Jesus

Appearance - Looking like, on the outside

Ash Wednesday - The first day of Lent, when we receive the ash on our foreheads

Assume - To take on as true

Attached - Joined

Banquet - Delicious meal or feast

Baptism - The first sacrament, by which a person becomes a Christian and joins the family of God

Betray - To break a promise to be loyal

Bishop - A priest who is in charge of all the people and churches of his area, that is, his diocese

Blessed Sacrament - The consecrated host, the body of Jesus, kept in the Tabernacle

Bond - Something that unites

Cherish - To care for tenderly

Civil rights - For example, someone's right to equality

Compassion - A feeling of concern that makes you want to help

Concentration camp - A guarded prison camp

Condemn/condemned - To decide someone is guilty

Confirmation - The sacrament by which a person receives the Holy Spirit to become a mature witness for Jesus

Consecration - At Mass when the Holy Spirit changes the bread and wine into the body and blood of Jesus

Contrite - Sorrowful

Convert - To make a complete change of heart

Crucifix - A cross with the figure of Jesus on it

Deacon - An ordained minister, who is not a priest

Decay - To rot and decompose

Defendant - Someone who has to defend themselves against what others are saying about them

Demons - Evil spirits; the devil

Discipleship - Following Jesus

Divinity - Of God, having the nature of God

Eternal life - The new life with God given at Baptism

Eucharist - The Mass, in which Jesus gives himself truly, under the appearance of bread and wine

Exodus - Journey of Israel from slavery to freedom

Expose/exposition - To put where everyone can see; adore the Blessed Sacrament

Fair trial - To treat a prisoner fairly in Court

Fair wages - The right amount of money to pay someone for the work they have done

Fellowship - The happiness God gives us being together with other people

Freedom - Ability to choose

Gentile - A person who was not born into the Jewish faith

Genuflect - To go down on one knee as a way of showing respect

Good Friday - The Friday in Holy Week, before Easter Sunday, when we remember the cucifixion and death of Jesus

Good News - The story of the life, death and resurrection of Jesus, also known as the Gospel

Grace - A help or gift which comes from God

Hallowed - Holy

Harmony - Peace

Holy Thursday - The Thursday before Easter, in Holy Week

Holy Week - The very special week for Christians leading up to Easter Sunday

Hospitality - Welcoming strangers

Host - The piece of unleavened bread that is used in Mass, to become the body of Jesus

Humanity - Of human beings, having the nature of human

Illegal - Against the law

Imitate - Copy

Imperfect - Not perfect

Infinite - Without end

Innocent - Not guilty; to have done nothing wrong

Inspirational - Makes you think of God and goodness

Inward grace - Help from God

Judaea - A Jewish region, south of Galilee, in Israel

Justice - Fairness

Kingdom values - The idea of right and wrong which God gives us when he comes to live in our lives and world

Law, The - Important rules which God gave to Moses

Leisure - Recreation time

Liturgy - Worshipping God in public prayer - ceremonies in Church for example

Memorial - Something that reminds you of someone or something

Messiah - The person God promised to send to save his people, that is Jesus

Miracle - Something extraordinary that happened through a supernatural power

Mission - Teaching or preaching the word of God

Monstrance - The gold or silver container for the Blessed Sacrament, used for adoration

Mysterious - something of God that is difficult to explain or understand

Nazarene - Someone who comes from Nazareth

New Covenant - The promises Jesus makes in the Gospels

Omission - Something we have failed to do

Opposition - When others are against you, or your ideas or beliefs

Orphan - A child that has lost both parents

Orphanage - A place where orphans are looked after

Our Lady - Mary, the mother of Jesus

Outward Sign - A visible symbol or action

Paradise - Another name for heaven

Passion - The suffering and death of Jesus

Pentecost - A Jewish feast 50 days after Passover; also a Christian feast 50 days after Easter

Pharisees - Strict religious Jews

Possessions - Things we own

Power on high - The power of God

Priest - Someone who has received the Sacrament of Ordination

Proclaim - To announce

Prophet - A holy person who hears God's word and tells others about it

Pure - Clean, without stain or badness

Racism/racist - To dislike someone because of their creed, race or colour

Reconciliation - Forgiveness

Religious - Men and women who dedicate their lives to God

Religious experts - People who know a lot about religion

Repent - To be sorry for sins and to make up for them

Resurrection - When Jesus rose from the dead on Easter Sunday

Reverence - To show great respect and love

Sabbath - The day of rest (Saturday for Jews, Sunday for Christians)

Sacramental sign - An outward sign of the sacrament

Sacrifice - To offer up something

Samaria - Region in Israel

Sanctuary lamp - A small lamp, usually red, placed near the Tabernacle, to remind us that God is truly present there

Sanitation - Clean and healthy water and sewerage facilities

Scribes - People who copy scripts

Segregation - To separate people from one another unjustly

Service - To help others

Shanty town - Where people live in shacks, with no proper housing

Tabernacle - Place in the Church where Jesus' body, the consecrated host, is held for worship

Talents - Gifts a person has

Trade Union - An organisation that looks after workers and represents them

Transform - Change

Trespasses - Old way of saying: wrongs we have done

Unique - One only; very special

Unleavened Bread - Bread that has been cooked without yeast, and so does not rise

Upper Room - The place where Jesus met his Apostles

Verdict - A decision about someone being innocent or guilty

Vocation - A particular calling from God

Vows - Very serious promises a person makes to God

Witness to - To be present

Zealous - To be very enthusiastic

Nihil obstat: Father Anton Cowan - Censor. **Imprimatur:** Rt Rev Alan Hopes, V.G. Auxiliary Bishop in Westminster, Westminster, 30 May 2004 Feast of Pentecost. *The* Nihil obstat *and* Imprimatur *are a declaration that the book or pamphlet is considered to be free from doctrinal or moral error. It is not implied that those who have granted the* Nihil obstat *and the* Imprimatur *agree with the contents, opinions or statements expressed.*

Acknowledgments
Considerable thanks are due to those teachers who commented on various drafts of this Pupil Book 6. The Way, the Truth and the Life Series has been a collaborative exercise: kind thanks are expressed to all those who have assisted. **Editorial Team:** Louise McKenna, Amette Ley, Elizabeth Redmond, Anthony O'Rourke, Laura Lamb, Joan McDonald, Denise Coen and Marcellina Cooney. **Professional Curriculum Adviser:** Margaret Cooling. **Theological Adviser**: Mgr Michael Keegan. **Musical Adviser**: Mike Stanley.